KETO DESSERTS
COOKBOOK

Easy, High-Fat, Low-Carb, Fat-Burning
Recipes, and Sweet Ideas for Your
Ketogenic Diet

MELISSA BAKER

When you start following the ketogenic diet, you may find that transitioning, in terms of finding good food to eat, is relatively easy. But for a lot of people, the most challenging part of this diet is giving up sweets. Does following the ketogenic diet and lifestyle mean that you have to say goodbye to desserts for the rest of your life?

Of course, not!

As you may have already guessed from the title of this book, enjoying desserts on while on keto isn't just possible—it's also part of the diet itself. Even if you can't find keto-friendly desserts in the bakeries, bakeshops, and cafes in your area, don't worry, we've got you covered! In this book, you will learn all about keto desserts and how to make them. Even if you're not a professional cook—or you don't have much experience with cooking or baking—you'll soon discover that when it comes to keto desserts, the options are endless.

Although sugar and other sugar-laden food items aren't recommended for maintaining a ketogenic state, there are specific ingredients you can use as alternatives for ingredients in traditional recipes. That way, you can continue eating these sweet treats without straying from your new diet. Making your own keto desserts means saying goodbye to carbs and processed sugar while saying hello to keto-baking staples such as:

- **Almond flour** that adds consistency, volume, and a nutty flavor.
- **Berries** that add color and natural sweetness.
- **Chocolate (sugar-free)**, the darker, the better!
- **Coconut flour** that binds, absorbs liquid and has a lovely tropical flavor.

INTRODUCTION:
Can You Enjoy Desserts on the Ketogenic Diet?

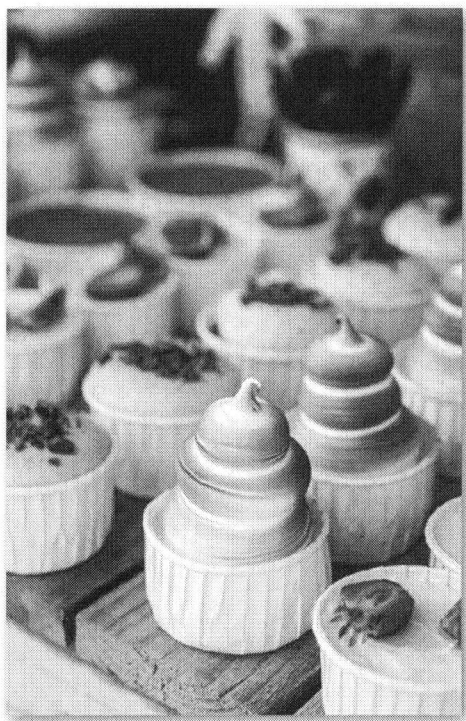

Contents

- **Dairy products (full-fat)** such as heavy whipping cream, cream cheese, butter, and more that add fullness, flavor, and creaminess.
- **Eggs** that bind and add more nutritional content.
- **Sweeteners** like erythritol, stevia, and others that will add guilt-free sweetness to your desserts.

When it comes to choosing ingredients for your recipes, always opt for sugar-free varieties when possible. This makes your desserts suitable for consumption even while on keto. Going sugar-free eliminates any excess sugars and carbs from your recipes. Otherwise, you may have to make some adjustments to the recipes if you can't find these sugar-free options. Don't worry, though, the more you practice creating keto desserts, the easier you'll be able to figure out proper adjustments to the recipes as needed.

Changing ingredients is the key to "ketofying" your desserts. After you've started making these recipes , search for your favorite traditional recipes, and see if you can make them more keto-friendly by replacing the necessary ingredients.

Learning how to cook and bake at home is an essential part of the ketogenic diet—especially if you plan on sticking with it long-term. The more practice, the easier it will be for you. You may also discover how enjoyable cooking is, especially after taking that first bite of the dish you've just cooked. Soon, you'll realize that you've leveled-up your skills from beginner to pro!

CHAPTER 1:
All About the Ketogenic Diet

THESE DAYS, THERE are so many different types of diets to choose from. Some surge in popularity but quickly fade away once people discover that they're either ineffective, unhealthy, or too difficult to follow. Then there are the other diets that keep growing more and more popular as people try them and see first-hand all of the benefits they offer.

The ketogenic diet is one such diet.

The ketogenic or simply, "keto" diet is one of the trendiest diets happening right now—and it looks like it's here to stay. The most basic definition of the ketogenic diet is it's a low-carb, high-fat diet that allows for moderate amounts of protein—and its main goal is to help your body reach a state of ketosis. Simple, right?

For some, this diet is very easy to follow. After all, it allows you to still eat butter, bacon, and other indulgent types of food. But if you're used to eating a lot of carbs and sweets, you might find this diet to be more of a challenge. Try thinking about your current diet (unless you're already on keto) and try to determine how different it is from the ketogenic diet. If you love pasta, rice, bread, and sweet stuff, brace yourself as you need to make a lot of changes to your diet. But if you're not fond of carbs and prefer whole foods or those which contain healthy fats, then making the transition to keto will be a breeze for you.

Either way, this diet is emerging in popularity—and for a good reason. It's incredibly effective, offers a lot of health benefits, and, despite being restrictive, the diet is easy to get used to. In fact, it has become so popular that some people are even combining keto with other kinds of diets and eating patterns such as veganism and intermittent fasting. And since you don't have to stop eating desserts while on keto, what's not to love about it?

While keto desserts are the main focus of this book, there is much more to know about this diet. Before we dive into the decadent dessert recipes, we're going to learn more about the ketogenic diet so you understand it better and feel more motivated to stick with it. Educating yourself about your diet makes you more aware of its effects as an important part of your life.

A Brief History of the Ketogenic Diet

The ketogenic diet initially gained its popularity in the 1920s, but it didn't get its start as a weight-loss regime. It was first recommended as part of the treatment for people suffering from epilepsy, but with the eventual emergence of anticonvulsant therapy, the ketogenic diet faded away. Eventually, though, doctors discovered that around 25% of patients didn't respond well to these new anticonvulsant therapies, particularly the young children. Because of this, doctors went back to recommending keto for the management of seizures.

It was only until the year 1911 when modern scientists started looking at the potential of fasting as part of the treatment of epilepsy. Back then, fasting was supposed to take the place of the use of potassium bromide, which had undesirable side effects such as slowing down the mental process. Compared to the utilization of potassium bromide, fasting, a restriction in the diets of patients, helped reduce the frequency of seizures while improving their mental ability. But since a lot of patients weren't able to stick with fasting or strict diet rules prescribed to them, they ended up going back to their diets.

In the year 1921, Rollin Woodyat, an endocrinologist, discovered that a low-carb, high-fat diet can help the liver produce ketones as the body reached a state known as "ketosis." This, in turn, was more beneficial to patients suffering from epilepsy. This new discovery pushed scientists to study this fact further, and in the same year, the term "ketogenic diet" was coined by Dr. Russel Wilder. After that, scientists started looking into the other health benefits of the ketogenic diet apart from being helpful to patients with epilepsy.

When they discovered that it was also beneficial for weight loss, this is when the diet really started to take off in popularity. It has now become a worldwide trend with its own following. As more and more people are becoming interested in going keto to lose weight and maintain blood sugar levels while still enjoying high-fat food options.

The Process of Ketosis

For most people—and most traditional diets—their primary energy source is sugar or glucose. But there is actually a more efficient energy source that is rarely used—ketones or ketone bodies. This energy source is used when the ketogenic diet is followed correctly, and a state of ketosis is reached.

Ketosis is a metabolic state of the body that occurs when there are high levels of ketones in the blood. Achieving this metabolic state is the central purpose of the ketogenic diet. Consuming a high-fat, moderate-protein, and low-carb diet induces the body into ketosis. This metabolic state is highly beneficial because it can help improve mood, mental performance, body composition, and more. It also helps in the prevention of disease, and it offers therapeutic benefits. When in ketosis, the body produces three types of ketone bodies which are:

- Acetone

- Acetoacetate (AcAc)
- Beta-Hydroxybutyrate (BHB)

Usually, human beings depend on using ketones for fuel when there aren't enough glucose sources. This is because ketosis is a normal process of the body, it's just not common for those who consume a lot of carbs and sugar. Because of the abundance of carbs in the diet, ketosis ends up becoming a dormant metabolic state. But once it is activated, the body can immediately adapt to using ketones for fuel instead of glucose.

The process of ketosis is actually very simple. Let's explain it in terms of the ketogenic diet. When you increase your consumption of fats, maintain a moderate intake of protein, and drastically restrict your carb intake, your body eventually runs out of glucose to burn. When this happens, it starts burning the fat you consume. Over time, your body becomes a capable fat-burning machine that burns the fat stored in your body. This is why weight-loss—more specifically, fat-loss—is one of the main benefits of the ketogenic diet.

CHAPTER 2:
Why Go Keto?

WHEN PEOPLE FIRST hear about the ketogenic diet and what it entails, they find its success rate hard to believe. After all, you have to eat fat to burn fat! When you look at it this way, it does seem far fetched and unlikely to work.

But as it turns out, increasing your intake of fats and bringing down your carb intake to a bare minimum is one of the fastest and most effective ways to lose weight. While this diet was originally developed to help medical patients, it has now gained recognition taken the world by storm. Starting on the ketogenic diet is like resetting your body for it to become a highly efficient fat-burning machine. The longer you stay in this diet, the more your body will continue burning fats.

If this isn't enough reason for you to go keto, you should know that unlike other diets out there, the effects and benefits of the ketogenic diet are supported by science. Because of how popular this diet is, more and more scientists and health experts have focused on studying it. Through these studies and research, they have discovered all the good things—and even the potential risks—of the wildly popular diet. And this is exactly what we will be discussing throughout this chapter.

The Benefits of the Ketogenic Diet

While some people are skeptical about the hype surrounding the keto diet, many researchers and experts swear that this is the best diet that exists today. Of course, there are still others who believe that this is just another "fad diet" that will soon lose its popularity. To some degree, either side can be considered correct. While the ketogenic diet is highly effective, it's not a perfect diet—because there is no such thing. Regardless, the ketogenic diet does offer several health benefits experienced by those who have been following the diet for some time now. If you're thinking about going keto, here are some benefits you may look forward to:

Weight-loss

This is one of the main advantages of the ketogenic diet, and clearly the most popular benefit. Losing weight is a natural consequence of following this diet correctly, especially when your body becomes a fat-burning machine. Achieving ketosis and maintaining it is essential for this benefit.

When you achieve ketosis, your insulin and blood sugar levels drop. When this happens, the fat cells in your body are able to release the water they have been retaining. This is why, in the beginning, most people lose a lot of weight—this is actually water weight. After this, the fat cells would be small enough to go into the bloodstream and into the liver so they can get converted into ketone bodies. This process continues as long as you follow the ketogenic diet correctly.

Higher energy levels

For most people, they will experience a sharp drop in energy levels at the beginning of this diet. This acts as an indication that your body is transitioning from burning glucose to burning fat. Once your body adapts, you will start feeling your energy levels rise. When the body uses fat as fuel, your endurance increases as well because this kind of fuel is more sustainable compared to glucose.

Beneficial for those who suffer from diabetes

Those who suffer from type I diabetes aren't able to produce enough insulin. This is why they need to deliver insulin externally. The good news is that going keto can help with the management of this condition. This is mainly because the ketogenic diet can help control the levels of blood sugar. In fact, studies have shown that this diet is the best one for those who suffer from type I diabetes. This is especially true if your keto diet is based on whole foods that provide healthy fats and nutrients.

This diet can be beneficial for those who suffer from type II diabetes as well. Research shows that shifting to the ketogenic diet can help normalize insulin levels and even reverse insulin resistance. Therefore, if you suffer from this condition, you may want to consult with your doctor and consider going keto.

Cravings and appetite reduce

When your blood sugar levels are stable, this helps control your cravings too. Because of this, you will be able to make better food choices because you're not just looking to satisfy your appetite. Also, you may notice that you don't feel as hungry as you used to in the past. This is why a lot of people will combine keto with intermittent fasting.

A reduction of inflammation

Following a low-carb diet can help reduce inflammation as this promotes nutritional ketosis. And when this happens, it also lowers your risk of developing other conditions such as arthritis, heart disease, autoimmune conditions, and more.

An improvement in sleep and sleep quality

Many keto followers have noticed that they fall asleep faster, and they achieve a deeper sleep each night. Although you might not experience this benefit right away, you will once your body has adjusted to ketosis and is continuously burning fat. When this happens, you will be able to enjoy a longer and deeper sleep, so you feel rested and restored when you wake up.

Improves the levels of HDL cholesterol and blood pressure

HDL is the good type of cholesterol that carries cholesterol to your liver for reuse or excretion. While on keto, your HDL cholesterol levels increase which, in turn, lower your risk for heart disease.

The same thing goes for blood pressure levels. Studies have shown that the ketogenic diet can help lower your levels of blood pressure. Although it's a high-fat diet, the restriction of carbs is what causes this benefit.

Brain benefits

When your brain runs on ketones instead of glucose, this may help maintain neuronal function, prevent the loss of neurons, and protect the brain cells against injuries. All these benefits help improve the health of your brain. Several studies have shown that when your brain runs on ketones, it functions more effectively. This means that you may notice your mind getting sharper over time.

In line with this, since the ketogenic diet improves the health of your brain, it may also prevent the development of neurodegenerative diseases such as Alzheimer's and Parkinson's diseases. It can even help reduce the occurrence of migraines, which is great news if you're a migraine sufferer.

Potential Side Effects of the Ketogenic Diet

While the ketogenic diet does offer a lot of health benefits, it also comes with some possible side effects. As with any other diet, the ketogenic diet might not be suitable for some people—such as for pregnant or nursing women, children, those who suffer from specific medical conditions, or those who are taking certain medications. Also, it's important to note that this diet is quite strict and restrictive. Unless you follow it correctly, you won't be able to reach—and maintain—ketosis. This means that you won't be able to enjoy all the benefits as well.

This is why it's important to learn everything you can about the ketogenic diet before following it. That way, you can determine whether you can follow it long-term or not. Now that you know the benefits of this diet, let's go through the potential side effects to look out for:

Keto flu

This is the most common side effect of the keto diet. The further your current diet is from keto, the higher the likelihood that you would experience keto flu. The symptoms of keto flu include dizziness, fatigue, insomnia, brain fog, and other signs of normal flu. Fortunately, this condition will go away in a few days.

For prevention, it's vital to ensure that you're always well-hydrated. Also, try to focus on whole, healthy, nutrient-dense foods, especially at the beginning of your diet. That way, your body will be strong enough to combat any viruses so you won't suffer through it for very long.

Severe muscle loss

This side effect may occur when you continue performing high-intensity exercises while following the ketogenic diet. You might experience severe muscle loss if you aren't getting enough protein in your diet. There is a variation of the ketogenic diet known as a

High-Protein Ketogenic Diet that allows you to eat more protein to sustain your workouts and active lifestyle.

Bowel movement changes

Since you would have to eliminate starchy foods from your diet, this would include several types of fruits and vegetables. Unfortunately, these high-fiber foods are the ones that keep your bowel movements regular. Unless you make sure that you still get enough fiber, you might have difficulties in having bowel movements which, when left unchecked, can lead to constipation.

Negative effects on the kidneys

This is a well-noted potential side effect of the high-fat diet. This is especially risky when you consume a lot of processed meats instead of focusing on whole foods and other healthier food items. Consuming a lot of animal proteins increases uric acid and calcium levels while making your urine more acidic too. These effects make you more susceptible to the development of kidney stones. Therefore, if you suffer from any kind of kidney disease, consult with your doctor first before going keto.

Dehydration

We have already discussed the fact that when you start on the keto diet, your body's fat cells will release a lot of water in the process. Apart from this, your kidneys will also release significant amounts of electrolytes when you experience a drop in your insulin levels. In the beginning, you may experience a significant drop in your weight—most of which is water. Unless you replenish your system by drinking a lot of water, you may experience dehydration as a side effect of your new diet.

Bad breath

When your body produces ketones by burning fat, it employs different methods to eliminate these ketones from the body—and one way is through respiration. When your lungs excrete ketones, they come out as acetone which has a foul smell. Therefore, you might notice that you have bad breath while your body is in ketosis. To reduce this risk, make sure to drink a lot of water. You may also turn to sugar-free gum or mints to alleviate this situation.

Possibility of nutrient deficiencies

This is another dangerous side effect to look out for. When you restrict entire food groups from your diet, this may lead to one type of nutrient deficiency or another. This is why it's essential to count your macros while following this diet. Also, you may have yourself tested regularly to ensure that you're getting all of the nutrients your body needs to stay healthy.

It might cause yo-yo dieting

Finally, the ketogenic diet may also cause you to start "yo-yo dieting." This is when you don't stick with your diet because you have already experienced some of the benefits. This is most common in terms of weight loss. After losing weight, you may go back to your old eating habits. Unfortunately, when you do this, it might also cause you to regain all of the weight back. Then you go back on keto, and the cycle starts all over again. To avoid this, try to stick with the diet for as long as you can.

CHAPTER 3:
Do's, Don'ts, and More

THE KETOGENIC DIET may seem complicated, but it doesn't have to be. This is why educating yourself about the diet is important. The more you know about keto and how to follow it, the more you will be able to understand what it involves and how you can follow it. In fact, with all the information you learn, you can even come up with your own customized plan for following the ketogenic diet. That way, you don't feel pressured with all the rules of the diet because you have come up with your own strategies!

As with any other diet, the ketogenic diet will take some getting used to. If your current eating habits are similar to keto, then you might not have to make a lot of changes. If not, then you can try easing into the diet gradually instead of trying to do too much, too fast. Usually, the challenges come at the beginning, but over time, you will either get used to them or overcome them. In this chapter, we will go through some helpful information to guide you on your keto journey. Use this information to come up with your own plan for starting—and sticking with—the ketogenic diet.

Foods to Eat on Keto

The ketogenic diet is quite strict in terms of the types of foods to eat (and avoid) for you to achieve ketosis. In the beginning, you might not be able to identify which foods you can eat right away. But the longer you stick with the diet, the more you will be able to determine whether a specific type of food or dish is keto or not. Also, it may be helpful for you to print out a list of recommended foods and foods to avoid. That way, you can refer to the list when meal prepping, cooking, or even ordering food. To start you off, here's a list of foods you can eat on keto:

Alcohol

While alcoholic drinks aren't recommended on keto, especially during your transition phase, this doesn't mean that you need to completely eliminate alcohol from your life. In fact, most types of liquor are keto-friendly because they contain minimal to no carbs at all. To maintain ketosis, here are some alcohol options for you:

- brandy
- cognac
- gin
- rum
- scotch
- tequila
- vodka
- whiskey

Beverages

The best beverage to drink while on keto is water. Have it with ice, sparkling or flat. Enjoy your water hot or infused with natural flavorings such as sliced lemons, limes, or cucumbers. Also, water can help you avoid or overcome the potential side effects of the ketogenic diet.

Coffee and tea are also great beverages to enjoy on the keto diet. For coffee, don't add any sugar but you may add a small amount of cream or milk. You can even add coconut oil or butter to make "Bulletproof coffee," a healthy way to add fats to your diet. As for tea, you can enjoy any type of tea as long as you don't add sugar to it.

Bone broth is another excellent option that's satisfying, hydrating, and filled with electrolytes and nutrients. It's easy to make bone broth at home for you to sip whenever you're feeling hungry or thirsty. For an energy boost, add a pat of butter to your hot bone broth.

Other beverages you can enjoy on keto include:

- coconut milk (diluted)
- nut milk (bottled)
- yerba mate

Dairy

When it comes to dairy products, butter is the best. You can also enjoy some high-fat cheeses on their own or added to your dishes. Just try not to snack on cheese a lot as this might prevent you from losing weight. For high-fat yogurts, you can enjoy these in moderation. When cooking, it's best to use heavy cream.

Fruits

Fruits are an essential part of the diet as they are healthy, and contain a lot of fiber. Unfortunately, there are a lot of fruits that are high in starches and sugars. When it comes to fruits, the best ones for your diet are lemons, limes, avocados, cranberries, coconut, and low-fructose berries. You may also enjoy other low-carb fruits on occasion.

Nuts, Seeds, and Legumes

You can have these in moderation as long as you're aware of how much you are eating. Because of this, it's not recommended to consume nuts and seeds as snacks as you might not notice that you've already had a lot of them. On occasion, you may enjoy hazelnuts, pecans, walnuts, macadamia nuts, and almonds. Also, you may use nut and seed flour for baking instead of starchy flour options.

Oils and Fats

When it comes to the keto diet, fat will make up most of your caloric intake. Therefore, you need to incorporate different types of healthy fats into your diet to ensure that you meet your daily fat requirement. Some of the best fats and oils for the keto diet include:

- avocado oil
- bacon fat (pastured)
- brain octane oil
- cacao butter
- coconut oil
- cod liver oil
- egg yolk (pastured)
- fish oil
- krill oil
- lard (pastured)
- marrow (pastured)
- MCT oil
- sunflower lecithin
- tallow (pastured)
- virgin coconut oil

Some fats and oils that you can enjoy on occasion include:

- chicken fat
- duck fat
- goose fat
- nut oils

Protein

The best types of meat are unprocessed. If you're looking for a healthier option, go for grass-fed, organic meat. But when it comes to protein, you must make sure that you only consume moderate amounts. Consuming too much protein might kick your body out of ketosis because excess protein gets converted into glucose. For the keto diet, most types of fish and seafood are suitable, but it's best to opt for fattier fish. You can enjoy eggs in any way as eggs contain both protein and cholesterol. Other protein sources include:

- colostrum
- collagen peptides
- dark meat
- gelatin
- organ meat
- pork
- whey protein concentrate
- On occasion, you may enjoy:
- chicken (pastured)
- turkey
- beef
- whey protein isolate

Spices, Seasonings, and Sauces

What would your dishes be without spices, seasonings, and sauces? These add flavor to your meals, and they can also add essential nutrients as long as you choose them well. For these types of food, you can enjoy:

- apple cider vinegar
- coconut aminos
- cocoa powder
- Ceylon cinnamon
- cilantro
- mustard
- ginger
- sea salt
- salad dressings
- oregano
- turmeric
- thyme
- vanilla bean

Also, you can occasionally enjoy:

- black pepper
- paprika
- garlic
- onion
- nutmeg

Sweeteners

Sugar isn't allowed on the ketogenic diet, but there are certain sweeteners that you can use as substitutes for sugar—especially for baking. These include:

- erythritol
- allulose
- stevia
- birch xylitol
- maltitol
- sorbitol

- monk fruit

Vegetables

Most vegetables—whether frozen or fresh—are fine on the keto diet. But the most recommended ones are leafy greens. From salads to stews, and more, veggies add a lot of flavor, variety, and essential nutrients to your diet. Some of the best vegetable options for the keto diet are:

- broccoli
- cabbage
- cauliflower
- zucchini
- asparagus
- bitter greens
- bok choy
- Brussels sprouts
- celery
- collards
- chard cucumbers
- endive
- kohlrabi
- kale
- lettuce
- nori
- radish
- olives
- summer squash
- spinach

On occasion, you can also enjoy these veggies:

- artichokes
- eggplant
- celery root
- green beans
- leeks
- jicama
- okra
- pumpkin
- parsnip
- peppers
- rhubarb
- tomatillo
- tomato
- winter squash
- turnip

Foods to Avoid on Keto

As you can see, there are a lot of food options to choose from while following the ketogenic diet. However, there is also a long list of foods to avoid—and this is where some people feel challenged. To give you a better idea of what you need to limit or eliminate from your diet, here's a list for you:

Alcohol

Many diets don't recommend the consumption of alcohol. The main reason for this is that excessive alcohol consumption isn't healthy. For the ketogenic diet, most types of alcohol are suitable—but this doesn't mean that you should freely consume alcoholic drinks that don't contain carbs. Remember, you should take care of your health to avoid experiencing the common side effects of the ketogenic diet. However, when it comes to alcohol, the types to avoid are:

- beer
- cider
- cocktails
- liqueurs

Beverages

For beverages, it's generally recommended to avoid high-sugar drinks like juices, energy drinks, any type of sodas, and more. Even fresh juices should be avoided, especially when made from fruits with high sugar and carb contents.

Dairy

While on keto, avoid all fake butter products, fake cheese products, and all low-carb dairy products. Milk isn't recommended for the ketogenic diet too because it's quite high in lactose sugar. Also, stay away from low-fat or sweetened dairy products like yogurt, buttermilk, and condensed or evaporated milk.

Fruits

Although fruits are healthy, a lot of them contain high amounts of sugar and carbs. Of course, this doesn't make them suitable for your new diet. Here are some examples of fruits you must avoid while on keto:

- apples
- oranges
- bananas
- watermelon
- grapes
- peaches
- pineapple
- melon
- cherries
- pears
- grapefruits

- mango
- plums

Nuts, Seeds, and Legumes

These foods are great fat sources, but they do contain a lot of proteins and fats too. And since it's easy to overeat nuts, seeds, and legumes, these other macros can add up quickly. Here are some examples you must avoid while on keto:

- black soybeans
- chia seed
- Brazil nuts
- edamame
- hemp seeds
- flaxseed
- chestnuts
- peanuts
- pistachios
- cashews
- pine nuts
- sunflower seeds

Oils and Fats

Oils and fats are recommended on the ketogenic diet, but this doesn't mean that all types are suitable. Here are some examples of oils and fats you must avoid while on keto:

- canola oil
- corn oil
- cottonseed oil

- flaxseed
- safflower
- commercial lard
- peanut
- soy
- sunflower oil
- low-carb dressings
- margarine
- hydrogenated fats
- trans fats
- polyunsaturated fats
- processed vegetable oils

Protein

It's important to moderate your consumption of proteins while on the keto diet. Because of this, you must choose your protein sources carefully. Opt for natural, whole protein sources as these are healthier. Here are some examples of proteins you must avoid while on keto:

- farmed seafood
- factory-farmed meats
- packaged, heavily processed meats
- protein powders from animals which are grain-fed
- soy protein

Spices and Seasonings

When cooking, baking, and meal prepping, spices, and seasonings are essential as these add flavor to your dishes. However, you must check the ingredients of these spices and seasonings to ensure that they are suitable for your diet. Stay away from those which contain added sugars and high-carb ingredients. Here are some examples of spices and seasonings you must avoid while on keto:

- artificial flavors
- spice extracts and mixes
- bouillon
- fermented tamari
- MSG
- soy products
- nutritional yeast
- all types of vinegar except apple cider vinegar
- spice blends that contain milk solids, sugars, corn starch, potato starch, or MSG
- table salt

Starch

Some starchy foods aren't suitable for the ketogenic diet because consuming these won't allow you to achieve ketosis. Remember, ketosis will only happen when you "starve" your body of sugar, carbs, and starches. This is one of the more difficult types of foods to avoid for a lot of people. Here are some examples of starchy foods you must avoid while on keto:

- bread

- rice
- pasta
- French fries
- potatoes
- sweet potatoes
- potato chips
- muesli
- porridge
- whole-grain products
- oats
- flour

Sugar and Sweeteners

Although there are a lot of keto-friendly desserts you can enjoy, all other sweets, sweeteners, and sugars aren't allowed while on keto. This is another broad category since keto is all about cutting down on glucose. Here are some examples of sweet foods, sugary foods, you must avoid while on keto:

- aspartame
- sucralose
- tagatose
- saccharin
- acesulfame
- sorbitol
- fructose
- honey
- agave
- maple syrup
- liquid sucralose
- sweets

- cakes
- candy
- cookies
- donuts
- chocolate bars
- frozen treats
- breakfast cereals
- sugar
- ice cream
- pastries

Vegetables

As with fruits, be careful with vegetables. While there are more options when it comes to veggies, there are a few starchy veggies that might sneak carbs into your diet without you knowing! Here are some examples of vegetables you must avoid while on keto:

- cruciferous veggies (raw)
- low-carb, canned vegetables
- mushrooms
- root vegetables
- leeks
- pumpkin
- parsnips
- rutabaga
- carrots
- parsnips
- yams
- yuca
- turnips
- beets

Keto Dessert FAQs

Knowing the types of food to eat and avoid on the keto diet is one thing—but having the willpower to avoid the things you used to love is another thing. Fortunately, the keto diet doesn't prevent you from eating ALL kinds of desserts. When it comes to desserts, the key is to "ketofy" them by switching up some of the ingredients. But before we go through the different keto dessert recipes, let's answer some of the most common dessert-related FAQs to help you better understand what eating desserts on the keto diet mean.

What should you do when you crave sweets on keto?

Craving sweets is normal, especially at the beginning of your keto journey. Although these cravings will go away the longer you stick with the diet, it can be a challenge when you're experiencing a craving, and you know that you can't give in. For this problem, the best thing you can do is bake yourself some keto-friendly desserts and sweet treats!

What does it mean to bake bread according to ketogenic guidelines?

This simply means that you would bake bread and other baked goods using ketogenic ingredients. The great thing about this is that when it comes to baking, you can make almost any kind of food item by just making alterations to the list of ingredients. That way, you can enjoy the fruits of your labor without feeling guilty.

Why are ketogenic desserts healthier?

Ketogenic desserts are a lot healthier than traditional desserts because they are made of healthier ingredients. For instance, instead of using wheat-based flour, you would use almond flour. Or instead of using refined sugar, you would use natural sweeteners. Since you will be using healthier ingredients to make your desserts, this makes the end-result healthier too.

What is insulin, and why is this important when it comes to desserts?

For us, insulin is one of the most important hormones. The pancreas secretes insulin, and it has an effect on carbohydrate metabolism and body fat. Basically, insulin is a storage hormone that moves nutrients from the bloodstream and transports them into the target tissues. Another role of insulin is to regulate your levels of blood sugar.

When eating carbs, the body needs to produce more insulin so that it can keep up with the high glucose levels in the bloodstream. However, consuming too many carbs too frequently may lead to insulin resistance and diabetes. But when you follow the ketogenic diet—including keto-friendly desserts—your body doesn't need to produce a lot of insulin, thus, reducing your risk of developing these conditions.

Do ketogenic desserts cause a spike in the levels of blood sugar?

Since ketogenic desserts require natural sweeteners and sugar substitutes, this means that they are low on the glycemic index. Therefore, even when you consume such sweets, your body can absorb them more gradually. This means that your blood sugar levels rise slowly as well instead of causing spikes in your blood sugar levels.

Why is almond flour a common ingredient in ketogenic desserts?

Later, you will see that a lot of the dessert recipes have almond flour as one of their ingredients. This is a common ingredient in keto baking because it's highly nutritious and it's low in carbs. Almond flour contains vitamin E—a type of antioxidant—and magnesium—a nutrient that enhances insulin function. Almond flour is also linked with lower levels of blood pressure and LDL cholesterol.

Do keto desserts still have a sweet taste?

Desserts wouldn't be desserts unless they tasted sweet, right?

The difference is that these desserts are made with healthier sweeteners making them suitable for the ketogenic diet.

Can vegans and vegetarians enjoy keto desserts too?

Of course! Practically anyone can enjoy keto desserts as long as they aren't allergic to any of the ingredients. Even in this case, all you would have to do is replace or omit the ingredient/s you're allergic to before making the dessert.

Keto Tips to Help You Get Started

The ketogenic diet isn't just trendy—it also happens to be one of the most unique diets out there. It combines the health benefits of nutritional ketosis with the effectiveness of calorie restriction to improve one's overall health and wellbeing. Whether you're interested in going keto or you have already started this diet, here are some tips to help you out:

Come up with a plan for your diet

Now that you know more about the ketogenic diet, you are also aware that it does come with some fairly strict rules. Therefore, it may be beneficial for you to come up with your own plan for how you will follow this diet. There are many things to think about when it comes to this diet. The foods to eat, the foods to avoid, whether or not you would like to start meal planning, ketogenic food options in your area, and more.

You need to consider all of this as you create your

plan to make it easier for you to strategize and motivate yourself to stick with your decision to go keto. A critical aspect of this is to decide what type of ketogenic diet to follow. This would depend on your own needs, preferences, and the kind of diet you think you can sustain long-term.

Clean up your environment

This is one of the easiest and best things you can do to increase your success. Once you have made a choice to go keto, it's time to clean up your space. This means that you should check all of the foods in your kitchen and remove everything that doesn't fit into your new diet.

You don't have to throw out these food items, especially if they aren't spoiled and you have a lot of non-keto food items. After sorting the foods in your kitchen, you can donate everything you don't need. Doing this allows you to make a fresh start so you can shop for keto-friendly food items and ingredients. Also, getting rid of non-keto foods in your home is essentially getting rid of the temptation to eat foods that you aren't part of your diet.

Prepare and plan for the potential side effects

We've gone through the possible side effects of this diet. So as not to feel demotivated, you may want to come up with a plan to either prevent these side effects or deal with them. Take, for instance, the keto flu. If you keep yourself well-hydrated and you focus on whole, healthy foods, you may be able to prevent this. But even if you do experience keto flu, you should know how to overcome it easily. The good news is that you already know about keto flu and that you can deal with it the same way as you would regular flu. Planning for these potential side effects makes it easier for you to protect yourself from them.

Drink a lot of water to remain hydrated

This is one of the most important things you should do when starting and following the ketogenic diet. Since your body will be going through some changes, you must drink a lot of water to ensure that you're always healthy and hydrated. This is especially important when you're sweating a lot or after working out.

Get enough sleep

When you have poor sleeping habits, this increases your body's production of stress hormones. This, in turn, makes it more difficult for you to achieve ketosis. Conversely, when you maintain a regular sleep schedule, and you get enough sleep each night, this helps enhance the potential health benefits of the ketogenic diet.

Move more!

This tip can help you overcome the potential side effects of the ketogenic diet such as muscle aches, low energy, and even the keto flu—especially at the beginning of your diet. Performing light exercises through the discomfort you feel may help you achieve ketosis more rapidly as you would be burning your existing glucose stores.

Consume more salt

Following the keto diet lowers your insulin levels. When this happens, your body also ends up excreting more salt because of the absence of carbs that cause spikes in insulin and retain sodium. While on keto, you may want to add around 3 to 5 grams of salt to your daily intake to help prevent electrolyte imbalances. You can do this by drinking bone broth, sprinkle more salt on meals, and eating low-carb food items that contain sodium.

Improve your gut health

Your gut health plays an important role in all the other systems of your body. This means that improving your gut health also improves your metabolic flexibility, cognitive functions, insulin sensitivity, hormone production, and more. This has an effect on how fast and how well your body will be able to transition from burning glucose to burning fat for fuel. The healthier your gut is, the easier it will be for your body to adapt to the ketogenic diet.

Always check the nutrition labels of food

When you go keto, you should make it a habit to check the nutrition labels. This doesn't just mean that you would read the labels. Instead, it means that you should really find out what the food items are made of. Doing this makes it easier for you to spot hidden carbs, sugars, and other ingredients that aren't suitable for your diet. When it comes to commercial food items, the most common products that may contain hidden carbs are:

- Low-carb food items like snacks, desserts, and treats.
- Spice blends.
- Berries and fruits.
- Tomato-based food items like tomato sauce, tomato paste, and others.
- Commercial condiments.
- Chiles and peppers.
- Diet soda.
- Chocolate.
- Some types of medications.

Avoid following the "dirty keto" diet

Dirty keto means that you consume a lot of low-quality, unhealthy or processed foods—as long as you follow the daily macronutrient ratios the keto diet requires. Obviously, this isn't the best way to go keto as there's a likelihood that you wouldn't experience all the health benefits this diet has to offer. Instead, you should opt for natural, whole, nutrient-dense foods that will improve your health and help you maintain ketosis.

Consider combining keto with IF after some time

The keto + IF combination is becoming more and more popular and for a good reason. This diet combination is easy to do—especially after you have already transitioned to the ketogenic diet successfully. Keto and IF complement each other because they offer similar benefits. This means that when following them together, the benefits they offer are enhanced.

Cook your own meals

Cooking your own meals saves you time, money, and gives you the assurance that everything you eat is keto-friendly. Right now, there are so many resources out there to help out in terms of ketogenic meals. But since this book is all about keto-friendly desserts, we've got you covered. Now that you know more about the ketogenic diet, it's time to get down to baking!

CHAPTER 4:
Delicious Keto Cookie Recipes

Now THAT YOU know more about the ketogenic diet and how you can still enjoy desserts while following this unique diet, it's time to start learning some simple, easy, and tasty recipes that will make your ketogenic journey more enjoyable. In this chapter, you will discover a number of cookie recipes that you can enjoy for dessert, as a snack or at any time of the day. Read on!

Butter Pecan Cookies

These cookies are buttery, full of pecans, and oh-so-satisfying. They're sweet, crisp, and would be the perfect sweet bite after a high-fat meal.

Time: 32 minutes

Serving Size: 16 cookies

Ingredients:

- 1 tsp vanilla extract
- 2 tsp gelatin
- ⅓ cup coconut flour
- ⅔ cup keto-friendly sweetener (divided)
- 1 cup almond flour
- 1 cup pecans
- 1 stick of butter (salted, cold, sliced)

Directions:

- Preheat your oven to 350 °F and use parchment paper to line a cookie sheet.
- In a food processor, combine vanilla, gelatin, coconut flour, almond flour, butter, and half of the sweetener. Pulse until moist crumbs start to form.
- Add the pecans then continue pulsing until the pecans are chopped. You should start to see the dough coming together.
- Take the dough out of the food processor, divide into 16 pieces (the amount depends on what size you make your cookies), and roll each piece into a ball.
- Pour the rest of the sweetener in a dish. Place each of the dough balls into the sweetener and press down gently to form a cookie shape. Flip over and coat both sides with sweetener then place on the cookie sheet.
- Place the cookie sheet in the oven and bake for about 17 to 19 minutes until the edges turn golden.

Chocolate Chip Cookies

There aren't many things in this world better than homemade chocolate chip cookies. With this sugar-free recipe, you can still enjoy this classic dessert without breaking your diet.

Time: 15 minutes

Serving Size: 10 cookies

Ingredients:

- ⅛ tsp of baking soda
- 1 tsp vanilla extract (pure)
- 3 tsp milk (as needed)
- 2 tbsp coconut oil
- 2 tbsp erythritol (powdered)
- 3 tbsp chocolate chips (sugar-free)
- 1 cup almond flour (finely ground)
- salt

Directions:

- Preheat your oven to 325 °F and use parchment paper to line a cookie sheet.
- Combine the dry ingredients and stir well to ensure that there aren't any clumps.
- Add the wet ingredients and continue mixing until you've formed a dough.
- Divide the dough into 10 equal pieces, shape each piece into a cookie, and place them on the cookie sheet.
- Place the cookie sheet in the oven and bake the cookies for 10 to 12 minutes.
- Take the cookie sheet out of the oven and allow the cookies to cool before serving.

Chocolate Cookies with Macadamias

These cookies are so chocolatey and rich just like fudge brownies! Adding the macadamias increases the fat content and gives the cookies a crunchy texture.

Time: 20 minutes

Serving Size: 16 cookies

Ingredients:

- ½ tsp of baking soda
- 1 tsp vanilla extract
- 2 tbsp almond butter
- 2 tbsp cocoa powder (unsweetened)
- ¼ cup macadamia nuts (chopped)
- ½ cup butter (melted)

- ½ cup erythritol (granulated)
- 1 ½ cup almond flour
- 1 egg
- salt

Directions:

- Preheat your oven to 350 °F and use parchment paper to line a cookie sheet.
- In a bowl, combine all of the ingredients and mix well until you have a stiff dough. Be careful not to overmix.
- Divide the dough into 16 pieces, shape each piece into a cookie, and place on the cookie sheet.
- Place the cookie sheet in the oven and bake the cookies for about 15 minutes.
- Take the cookie sheet out of the oven and allow the cookies to cool completely before serving.

Cream Cheese Cookies

These cookies are easy to make, quick, and you can enjoy them in different ways. They're also a classic type of cookie you can make for your loved ones during the holidays.

Time: 25 minutes

Serving Size: 24 cookies

Ingredients:

- 2 tsp vanilla extract
- ¼ cup butter (softened)
- ¼ cup cream cheese (softened)
- ½ cup erythritol
- 3 cups almond flour (blanched)
- 1 large egg (white only)
- salt

Directions:

- Preheat your oven to 350 °F and use parchment paper to line a cookie sheet.
- Combine the erythritol, butter, and cream cheese in a bowl and beat together using a hand mixer until you have a fluffy, light-colored mixture.
- Beat the egg white, vanilla extract, and a pinch of salt into the mixture.
- Beat the almond flour into the mixture a half a cup at a time. Continue beating until you have a dough that's dense and slightly crumbly.
- Divide the dough into 24 pieces, shape each piece into a cookie, and place them on the cookie sheet.
- Place the cookie sheet in the oven and bake the cookies for 15 minutes.
- Take the cookie sheet out of the oven and allow the cookies to cool down completely before serving.

Fluffy Sugar Cookies

These cookies are soft, buttery, pillowy, and will surely satisfy your sweet cravings. Ending your meal with these cookies will make you feel happy and satisfied.

Time: 1 hour 15 minutes

Serving Size: 12 cookies

Ingredients:

- 1 tsp of baking powder
- 2 tsp vanilla extract
- 2 tbsp butter
- ½ cup keto-friendly sweetener
- ¾ cup cream cheese (full-fat)

- 1 cup almond flour
- 1 cup mozzarella cheese (shredded)
- 2 eggs (whites only)

Directions:

- In a microwave-safe bowl, combine the mozzarella and cream cheese. Melt the cheeses in 30-second intervals and mix well to combine thoroughly. For the next steps, you must work quickly.
- Add the baking powder, vanilla extract, butter, sweetener, almond flour, and egg whites to the bowl.
- Knead the dough with your hands to combine all of the ingredients well.
- Place the dough on a silicone mat, wrap with parchment paper, and chill in the refrigerator overnight.
- The next day, preheat your oven to 350 °F and use parchment paper to line a cookie sheet.
- Divide the dough into 12 pieces, shape each piece into a cookie, and place them on the cookie sheet.
- Place the cookie sheet in the oven and bake the cookies for 15 to 17 minutes.
- Take the cookie sheet out of the oven and allow the cookies to cool down before serving.

Fudgy Brownie Cookies

These brownie cookies are super fudgy and thick—but they're also gluten and sugar-free. To enhance the flavor, you can sprinkle some salt over the cookies after baking.

Time: 18 minutes

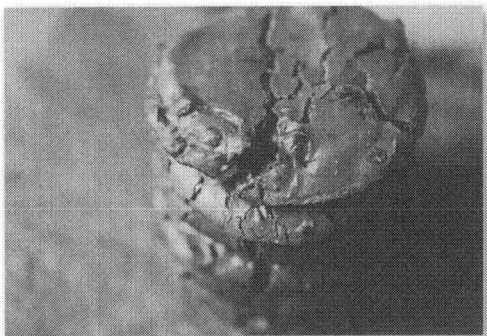

Serving Size: 10 cookies

Ingredients:

- 1 tsp of baking soda
- 1 tsp vanilla extract
- ⅓ cup coconut flour
- ½ cup chocolate chips (sugar-free)
- ½ cup cocoa powder
- ¾ cup butter (melted)
- ¾ cup xylitol
- 2 eggs (beaten)
- salt

Directions:

- Preheat your oven to 350 °F and use parchment paper to line a cookie sheet.
- In a bowl, combine coconut flour, butter, and xylitol. Add the eggs and use an electric mixer to mix all of the ingredients together.
- Add the vanilla extract, coconut flour, cocoa powder, and salt then continue mixing.
- Use a spatula to fold in the chocolate chips. By now you should have a very thick batter.
- Use a cookie scoop to scoop the batter onto your cookie sheet then press a few chocolate chips into the top of each cookie.
- Place the cookie sheet in the oven and bake the cookies for about 13 minutes.
- Take the cookie sheet out of the oven and allow the cookies to cool before serving.

Gingerbread Cookies

Making these gingerbread cookies requires very few ingredients plus a couple of spices. They are crispy and light on the outside, chewy on the inside, and have a classic flavor.

Time: 25 minutes

Serving Size: 10 cookies

Ingredients:

- ¼ tsp cloves (ground)
- ¼ tsp nutmeg
- ½ tsp of baking powder
- 1 tsp vanilla extract
- 1 ½ tsp ginger (ground)
- 1 tbsp cinnamon
- ¼ cup butter
- ¼ cup erythritol
- 2 cups almond flour (blanched)
- 1 big egg

Directions:

- In a bowl, combine the cloves, nutmeg, baking powder, ginger, cinnamon, and almond flour then mix well to incorporate.
- In a separate bowl, combine the erythritol and butter then beat with a hand mixer until fluffy. Add the vanilla extract and egg then continue beating.
- Add the mixture of dry ingredients and continue beating until it forms into a dough.
- Take the dough out of the bowl, form into a ball, and refrigerate for at least 30 minutes.
- Preheat your oven to 350 °F and use parchment paper to line a cookie sheet.
- Take the dough ball out of the refrigerator and roll it out until it's ¼-inches in thickness.
- Cut out cookie shapes with a gingerbread man cookie cutter and transfer each cookie on the cookie sheet.
- After cutting out all of the shapes, take the remaining dough, form into a ball, roll it out and cut out more cookies. Repeat this step until you've used all of the dough up.
- Place the cookie sheet in the oven and bake the cookies for about 10 to 15 minutes.
- Take the cookie sheet out of the oven and allow the cookies to cool down before handling or serving.

Keto Oreos

If you love Oreos, you'll love this recipe. Just because you've gone keto, doesn't mean that you have to give up your favorites!

Time: 1 hour (chilling not included)

Serving Size: 12 cookies

Ingredients for the cookies:

- ½ tsp of baking powder
- 1 tsp vanilla extract (pure)
- 2 tbsp coconut flour
- ⅓ cup of cocoa powder (black)
- ⅓ cup keto-friendly sweetener (granulated)
- ⅓ cup of vegetable oil
- ¾ cup almond flour
- 1 large egg
- kosher salt

Ingredients for the filling:

- 1 tsp vanilla extract (pure)

- ¾ cup keto-friendly sweetener (powdered)
- 1 stick of butter (softened)

Directions:

- In a bowl, combine the baking powder, coconut flour, cocoa powder, sweetener, almond flour, and a pinch of salt then mix well.
- Add the vanilla extract, vegetable oil, and egg then continue mixing until well combined.
- Shape the dough into a ball, wrap with plastic wrap, and refrigerate until firm (about 2 hours).
- Preheat your oven to 350 °F and use parchment paper to line a cookie sheet.
- Dust a clean surface lightly with cocoa powder, place the dough ball and roll out until ¼-inches in thickness.
- Use a round cookie cutter to cut out the cookie shapes and place the cookies on the cookie sheet.
- Place the cookie sheet in the oven and bake the cookies for about 14 to 16 minutes until slightly firm.
- Take the cookie sheet out of the oven and set aside, allowing the cookies to cool.
- Use a hand mixer to beat the butter in a bowl until you get a smooth consistency.
- Add the sweetener, beat to combine well, and mix the vanilla extract in.
- Assemble your keto-Oreos. Take one cookie, spread some filling on one side, and sandwich the filling with another cookie. Repeat this process with the rest of the baked cookies.

Lemon Sugar Cookies

Simple as these cookies are to make, they will surely become one of your favorites. The lemon glaze and sanding "sugar" give these cookies a unique, fresh taste.

Time: 25 minutes
Serving Size: 24 cookies

Ingredients for the cookies:

- ½ tsp xanthan gum
- 1 tsp of baking powder
- 3 tbsp lemon juice (fresh)
- 6 tbsp butter
- ¼ cup coconut flour
- ½ cup keto-friendly sweetener (powdered)
- 1 ½ cups almond flour
- 1 large egg
- 1 lemon (zest only)
- salt

Ingredients for the sanding sugar:

- 2 tbsp keto-friendly sweetener (granulated)
- 1 drop food coloring (gel, yellow)

Ingredients for the lemon glaze:

- 3 tbsp lemon juice (fresh)
- 6 tbsp keto-friendly sweetener (powdered)

Directions:

- Make the sanding sugar by combining both ingredients. Mix well to incorporate the food coloring into the sweetener granules then set aside.
- In a bowl, combine xanthan gum, baking powder, coconut flour, almond flour, and a pinch of salt then whisk well.
- In a separate bowl, combine the sweetener and butter then beat to mix well. Beat in lemon juice, lemon zest, and egg.
- Add dry ingredients to the bowl and continue beating until the dough starts to form.
- Place the dough on a sheet of parchment paper, shape into a circle, and top with another sheet of parchment paper.
- Roll out the dough until it's about ¼-inches in thickness. Transfer to a baking sheet and place in the refrigerator for about 30 minutes to chill.
- Preheat your oven to 325 °F and use parchment paper to line a cookie sheet.
- Take the chilled dough out of the refrigerator and use a cookie cutter to cut out cookie shapes of your choice.

- Transfer the cookies on the prepared cookie sheet, making sure that they have at least ½-inch spaces between them.
- After cutting out all of the shapes, take the remaining dough, form into a ball, roll it out and cut out more cookies. Repeat this step until you've used all of the dough up.
- Place the cookie sheet in the oven and bake for about 12 to 14 minutes.
- Take the cookie sheet out of the oven and allow the cookies to cool down completely.
- In a bowl, combine ingredients for the glaze and mix until you get a smooth consistency.
- Spread the glaze thinly over each of the cookies and sprinkle with sanding sugar.

Peanut Butter Cookies

If you're a lover of peanut butter, you'll love these cookies. They're light and crisp on the outside and have a center that melts in your mouth.

Time: 15 minutes

Serving Size: 15 cookies

Ingredients:

- ½ tsp vanilla extract
- ½ cup golden erythritol
- 1 cup of peanut butter (salted, unsweetened)
- 1 egg
- kosher salt
- ½ tsp blackstrap molasses (optional)
- flaky sea salt (for garnish, optional)

Directions:

- Preheat your oven to 325 °F and use parchment paper to line a cookie sheet.
- In a bowl, combine the sweetener, egg, and

molasses (if desired) and whisk well until fluffy and light.

- Add the vanilla extract and peanut butter. Continue whisking until you get a crumbly mixture. Also, add a pinch of kosher salt.
- Divide the dough into 15 pieces, form into rough cookie shapes, and use a fork to press down on the center.
- Place the cookies on the cookie sheet and place in the freezer for about 15 minutes before baking.
- After freezing, place the cookie sheet in the oven and bake the cookies for about 12 to 14 minutes.
- If you want to garnish with flaky sea salt, do this halfway through the baking process.
- Take the cookie sheet out of the oven and allow to cool completely before serving.

Salted Caramel Cookies with Chocolate Chips

These chewy, rich, and healthy cookies are out of this world. Since they fit into your keto diet, you can enjoy them after your meals with zero guilt.

Time: 22 minutes

Serving Size: 18 cookies

Ingredients:

- 1 tsp of baking soda
- 1 tsp caramel extract
- 1 tsp vanilla extract
- 1 tbsp collagen gelatin (grass-fed)
- ½ cup of coconut oil (unrefined, melted)
- ½ cup maple syrup (sugar-free)
- 1 cup dark chocolate chips (sugar-free)
- 3 cups almond flour (blanched)
- 2 big eggs
- sea salt
- sea salt flakes (for garnish)

Directions:

- Preheat your oven to 375 °F and use parchment paper to line a cookie sheet.
- In a bowl, combine the baking soda, gelatin, almond flour, and a pinch of salt then mix well.
- In a separate bowl, add the eggs, caramel extract, and vanilla extract then whisk to combine. Continue whisking as you add the coconut oil and maple syrup.
- Add the mixture to the bowl of dry ingredients and use a hand mixer to incorporate everything well.
- Use a rubber spatula to fold in the chocolate chips.
- Scoop balls of batter onto the cookie sheet you have prepared and press down gently to flatten.
- Place the cookie sheet in the oven and bake the cookies for about 10 to 12 minutes.
- Take the cookie sheet out of the oven, sprinkle the cookies with sea salt flakes, and allow to cool for about 10 minutes before serving.

Shortbread Cookies

This is a sugar-free and low-carb take on the classic shortbread cookies. They're buttery, crumbly, and light with a coconut glaze that's deliciously rich.

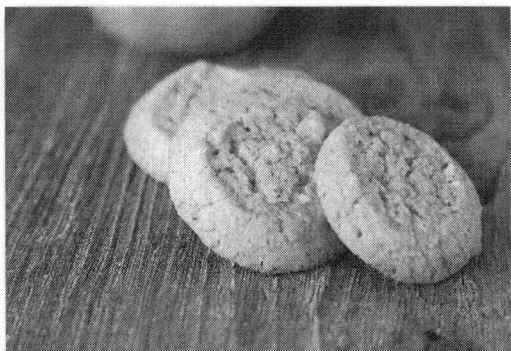

Time: 21 minutes

Serving Size: 20 cookies

Ingredients for the cookies:

- ¼ tsp of baking powder
- 1 tsp vanilla extract
- 2 tsp keto-friendly sweetener (powdered)
- ⅓ cup coconut flour
- ⅓ cup erythritol
- ½ cup butter (softened)
- ⅔ cup almond flour
- ¼ tsp xanthan gum (optional)

Ingredients for the glaze:

- 2 tsp keto-friendly sweetener (granulated)
- ¼ cup coconut butter

Directions:

- Preheat your oven to 350 °F and use parchment paper to line a cookie sheet.
- Combine all of the dry ingredients in a bowl and mix well.
- Add the vanilla extract, sweetener, and butter then continue mixing until you get a smooth dough.
- Divide the dough into two, roll out each piece between sheets of parchment paper, and place in the refrigerator for about 10 minutes.
- Take the dough out of the refrigerator, use a cookie cutter to cut out the desired cookie shapes, and place the cookies on the cookie sheet you have prepared.
- Place the cookie sheet in the oven and bake the cookies for about 6 minutes.
- Take the cookie sheet out of the oven and allow to cool before adding the glaze.
- Place the coconut butter in a microwave-safe container and warm in the microwave. Stir the sweetener in until you get a smooth texture.
- Spread the glaze lightly over each of the cookies and wait for it to set before serving.

Snickerdoodles

These cookies are perfectly light, tangy, soft, and full of that comforting cinnamon flavor. This low-carb, gluten-free recipe is another excellent addition to your diet.

Time: 20 minutes
Serving Size: 24 cookies

Ingredients for the cookies:

- ⅓ cup butter (unsalted, grass-fed)
- ⅓ cup erythritol
- ½ cup almond flour
- ½ tsp of baking soda
- ½ tsp cream of tartar
- ½ tsp xanthan gum
- 1 ½ tsp vanilla extract
- 2 tbsp coconut flour
- 1 egg
- kosher salt

Ingredients cinnamon sugar:

- 2 tsp cinnamon

- 2 tbsp erythritol

Directions:

- Preheat your oven to 350 °F and use parchment paper to line a cookie sheet.
- In a bowl, combine the almond flour, baking soda, cream of tartar, xanthan gum, coconut flour, and a pinch of salt. Whisk to combine thoroughly then set aside.
- In a separate bowl, use an electric mixer to cream the butter until softened. Add the erythritol and continue mixing until you get a fluffy and light mixture.
- Add the vanilla extract and egg then continue mixing until incorporated. You will have a mixture that appears "slightly broken," not smooth.
- Turn down the setting of your mixer on low and continue mixing as you add half of the dry ingredient mixture. After incorporating, add the rest of the mixture.
- Combine the cinnamon sugar ingredients and mix well.
- Use a spoon to scoop out the cookie batter, place each scoop on the cookie sheet, roll in the cinnamon sugar, and flatten the cookies to the desired thickness.
- Place the cookie sheet in the oven and bake the cookies for about 6 to 8 minutes.
- Take the cookie sheet out of the oven and allow the cookies to cool for about 10 minutes before serving.

Thin Mint Cookies

These sugar-free thin mints will tickle your taste buds in a new way. You can indulge in these palatable treats for dessert without all the carbs and sugar.

Time: 1 hour

Serving Size: 20 cookies

Ingredients for the cookies:

- ½ tsp vanilla extract
- 1 tsp of baking powder
- 2 tbsp butter (melted)
- ⅓ cup of cocoa powder
- ⅓ cup keto-friendly sweetener
- 1 ¾ cups almond flour
- 1 large egg (slightly beaten)
- salt

Ingredients for the coating:

- 1 tsp peppermint extract
- 1 tbsp coconut oil
- 1 cup dark chocolate (sugar-free, chopped)

Directions:

- Preheat your oven to 300 °F and use parchment paper to line a cookie sheet.
- In a bowl, combine the baking powder, cocoa powder, sweetener, almond flour, and a pinch of salt then mix well to incorporate.
- Add the vanilla extract, butter, and egg then continue mixing until dough forms.
- Roll the dough out until it's about ¼-inches in thickness.
- Use a cookie cutter to cut out the desired cookie shapes, lift them gently, and place the cookies on the cookie sheet you have prepared.
- After cutting out all of the shapes, take the remaining dough, form into a ball, roll it out and cut out more cookies. Repeat this step until you've used all of the dough up.
- Place the cookie sheet in the oven and bake the cookies for about 20 to 30 minutes.
- Take the cookie sheet out of the oven and allow the cookies to cool down and become crispy.
- In a pot, bring water to a boil, reduce the heat, and allow to simmer gently. Place a bowl made of metal over the pot, making sure that it doesn't touch the simmering water.

- Add the oil and chocolate to the bowl and stir continuously until smooth.
- Remove the bowl from the heat, add the peppermint extract, and stir.
- Dip each of the cookies in the melted chocolate completely, gently tap to remove any excess chocolate, and place on a baking sheet lined with wax paper.
- Place the baking sheet in the refrigerator to set.

Thumbprint Cookies

This keto-friendly dessert includes all the components of the classic thumbprint cookie. The pillowy, soft cookies are crusted with walnuts and have a dollop of jam in the center.

Time: 28 minutes

Serving Size: 15 cookies

Ingredients:

- ½ tsp of baking powder
- 1 tsp vanilla extract
- 5 tbsp strawberry preserves (sugar-free)
- ⅓ cup walnuts (finely chopped)
- ½ cup butter (salted, softened)
- ⅔ cup erythritol (powdered)
- 2 cups almond flour (blanched, superfine)
- 1 large egg (beaten)
- kosher salt

Directions:

- Preheat your oven to 375 °F and use parchment paper to line a cookie sheet.
- In a bowl, combine the baking powder, vanilla extract, butter, erythritol, almond flour, egg, and a pinch of kosher salt then mix well to form a dough.
- Prepare the walnuts by placing them in a shallow dish.
- Divide the dough into 15 pieces, form each of them into a ball, and roll in the dish of walnuts to thoroughly coat. Then place the coated cookies on the prepared cookie sheet and flatten slightly.
- Place the cookie sheet in the oven and bake the cookies for about 8 minutes.
- Take out of the oven, press a dent into the center of the cookies, and place a teaspoon of jam into the dent.
- Return the cookie sheet back in the oven and continue baking for 10 more minutes.
- Take the cookie sheet out of the oven, transfer the cookies to a platter, and allow to cool down for about 30 minutes before serving.

CHAPTER 5:
Delicious Keto Cake, Cupcake, and Muffin Recipes

KETO-FRIENDLY COOKIES ARE only the beginning. When it comes to keto desserts, there are endless possibilities—as long as you have the patience, drive, and interest in finding dessert recipes or even making your own after you've practiced with all of the simple but tasty recipes in this book. In this chapter, we will go through a few cake, cupcake, and muffin recipes to add to your keto dessert arsenal.

Cake Roll with Nutella

This Nutella cake roll is so delicious that you wouldn't even know that it's low-carb and healthier than traditional Nutella cakes. And the best part is—it's so simple to make!

Time: 2 hours

Serving Size: 1 cake roll

Ingredients for the Nutella filling:

- ½ tsp vanilla extract
- 1 tbsp cacao (powdered)
- 1 tbsp coconut oil
- 2 tbsp erythritol (powdered)
- ½ cup almonds
- 1 cup hazelnuts (peeled)
- 1 cup macadamia nuts
- 1 bar of dark chocolate (sugar-free)
- ½ cup coconut milk (optional)

Ingredients for the cake:

- ½ tsp vanilla extract
- ¾ cup erythritol (powdered)
- 1 cup mascarpone cheese
- 1 ½ cup almond flour
- 6 large eggs
- sea salt

Ingredients for the ganache:

- ½ tsp vanilla extract
- 3 tbsp butter
- ¼ cup plus 1 tbsp coconut milk
- 1 bar of dark chocolate
- keto-friendly sweetener (liquid, optional)

Directions:

- Preheat your oven to 375 °F and use parchment paper to line a baking tray.
- Spread the nuts on the baking tray, place the baking tray in the oven, and bake for 8 to 10 minutes.
- Take the baking tray out of the oven and allow the nuts to cool down for about 15 minutes.
- In a pot, bring water to a boil, reduce the heat, and allow to simmer gently. Place a bowl made of metal over the pot, making sure that it doesn't touch the simmering water.
- Add the oil and chocolate to the bowl and stir continuously until smooth. Take the bowl out of the heat and set aside.

- In a food processor, place the baked nuts and pulse until you get a smooth consistency.
- Add the chocolate, vanilla extract, cacao, erythritol, and coconut oil then continue pulsing. If you choose to add coconut milk, slowly drizzle it into the mixture while pulsing.
- Pour your Nutella mixture in a jar and allow to cool before storing in the refrigerator.
- Preheat your oven to 175 °F and use parchment paper to line a baking tray.
- Use a hand whisk to beat the eggs in a bowl until frothy.
- Add a pinch of salt and sift in the erythritol slowly while you beat the eggs.
- Fold in the vanilla extract and almond flour gently.
- Pour batter into the baking tray and spread evenly.
- Place the baking tray in the oven and bake the cake for about 8 to 10 minutes.
- Take the baking tray out of the oven, flip the cake onto another sheet of parchment and cover with a slightly damp kitchen towel. Allow cooling for about 3 minutes.
- After cooling slightly, peel off the parchment paper from the cake gently. Roll the cake tightly along with the parchment paper. Set aside to cool for a couple of minutes.
- In a bowl, mix equal amounts of mascarpone cheese and homemade Nutella.
- Unroll the cake gently and spread the filling

inside. Don't spread the mixture all the way to the edges to keep it from oozing when you roll.

- Start rolling the cake by with one hand while pulling off the parchment with the other. Place the cake in the refrigerator to cool while preparing the ganache.
- Break the bar of chocolate into pieces and place in a bowl.
- In a saucepan, heat the coconut milk and butter on medium-high heat.
- Once it starts foaming, slowly pour the liquid over the dark chocolate while continuously stirring. Doing this combines the ingredients well. Allow to cool for a few minutes.
- Take the cake out of the refrigerator and spread the ganache all over.
- Place the cake back into the refrigerator for a minimum of 20 minutes before you cut into it.

Chocolate Cake with Buttercream Frosting

This cake is intensely chocolatey and incredibly moist. It will be the perfect dessert to wrap up your meal. Whether you top it off with frosting or not, this cake is the bomb.

Time: 40 minutes

Serving Size: 1 cake

Ingredients for the cake:

- ¼ tsp xanthan gum
- ½ tsp espresso powder
- 1 tsp of baking powder
- 1 ½ tsp coconut flour
- 3 ½ tsp golden flaxseed meal (finely ground)
- 2 tbsp coconut cream
- 4 tbsp coconut oil
- ¼ cup almond flour
- ⅓ cup of cocoa powder

- ⅓ cup keto-friendly sweetener
- 2 eggs
- kosher salt

Ingredients for the frosting:

- 2 tsp vanilla extract
- ⅓ cup erythritol (powdered)
- ½ cup butter (unsalted, grass-fed)
- ½ cup cream cheese
- kosher salt

Directions:

- Preheat your oven to 375 °F, position a rack in the lower part of your oven, grease a cake pan, and dust it with cocoa powder.
- In a bowl, combine xanthan gum, baking powder, coconut flour, flaxseed meal, coconut flour, and almond flour then whisk until well-incorporated. Set aside.
- In a heatproof bowl, combine the espresso powder, coconut cream, coconut oil, cocoa powder, and a pinch of salt. Heat the mixture over a water bath while whisking constantly.
- Remove the bowl from the water bath, then set aside to cool for a bit.
- Add the sweetener and eggs one by one while you continue whisking until you get a thick and smooth mixture.
- Add the dry ingredient mixture while whisking until you've blended all of the ingredients together well.

- Pour the batter in the cake pan you have prepared.
- Place the cake pan in the oven and bake the cake for about 15 to 19 minutes. After 15 minutes, keep checking the cake to avoid overbaking.
- Take the cake pan out of the oven and allow the cake to cool down for about 30 minutes. Then transfer the cake to a rack.
- After cooling completely, place the cake in the refrigerator to chill while you prepare the frosting. You can also slice the cake horizontally before chilling if you plan to make a layered, frosted cake.
- In a bowl, combine the cream cheese and butter. Use an electric mixer to combine these ingredients evenly.
- Add the erythritol and a pinch of salt while you continue mixing. You should have a fluffy and pale mixture. Once fully incorporated, add the vanilla extract and continue mixing to combine.
- After your cake has chilled in the refrigerator, you can start applying the frosting however you wish. Then place back in the refrigerator to chill before serving.

Decadent Cheesecake

This low-carb, sugar-free cheesecake requires just a few ingredients, and you can make it in a matter of minutes. And the best part is—it tastes just like the real thing!

Time: 1 hour and 10 minutes

Serving Size: 1 cake

Ingredients for the crust:

- 1 tsp vanilla extract
- 3 tbsp erythritol
- ⅓ cup butter (melted)
- 2 cups almond flour (blanched)

Ingredients for the filling:

- 1 tbsp lemon juice (fresh)
- 1 tbsp vanilla extract
- 1 ¼ cups erythritol (powdered)

- 4 cups cream cheese (softened)
- 3 large eggs

Directions:

- Preheat your oven to 350 °F and grease a springform pan.
- Combine all of the crust ingredients in a bowl and mix well to combine. You will have a slightly crumbly mixture.
- Pour this mixture onto the springform pan you have prepared and press it into the bottom evenly.
- Place the springform pan in the oven and bake the crust for 10 to 12 minutes.
- Take the springform pan out of the oven and allow to cool for a minimum of 10 minutes.
- Use an electric mixer to beat the powdered sweetener and cream cheese together. Beat on medium speed until you get a fluffy consistency.
- Beat the eggs in one by one. Then beat the vanilla extract and lemon juice in.
- Pour the filling over the baked crust and use a spatula to smoothen the top.
- Place the springform pan back in the oven and continue baking for 45 to 55 minutes.
- Take the springform pan out of the oven and allow the cheesecake to cool down to room temperature. Once cooled, place the cheesecake in the oven for a minimum of 4 hours before serving.

Vanilla Pound Cake

This cake is a simple dessert that comes with an excellent macros content and just enough sweetness to round off your meal. Read on to learn how to make it!

Time: 1 hour and 5 minutes

Serving Size: 1 cake

Ingredients:

- 1 tsp vanilla extract
- 2 tsp of baking powder
- ¼ cup cream cheese
- ½ cup butter
- 1 cup erythritol (granulated)
- 1 cup sour cream
- 2 cups almond flour
- 4 large eggs

Directions:

- Preheat your oven to 350 °F and grease a bundt pan.
- In a bowl, combine the baking powder and almond flour, mix well, and set aside.
- In a microwaveable bowl, combine the cream cheese and butter. Microwave for 30 seconds while making sure that the ingredients don't burn.
- Take the bowl out of the microwave and stir the ingredients well to combine.
- Add the vanilla extract, sour cream, and erythritol then stir well.
- Add dry ingredients to the mixture and stir well. Add the eggs and continue stirring to incorporate.
- Pour cake batter into the bundt pan you have prepared.
- Place the bundt pan in the oven and bake the cake for about 50 minutes.
- Take the bundt pan out of the oven and allow the cake to cool down completely before taking it out.

Tiramisu

It might come as a pleasant surprise to you that you can still eat tiramisu while on keto. This dessert may take some time to make, but it will definitely be worth it!

Time: 4 hours and 20 minutes

Serving Size: 8 mini tiramisu cakes

Ingredients for the cake:

- 1 tsp of baking powder
- 4 tsp butter (salted)
- ½ cup almond flour
- 2 eggs

Ingredients for the tiramisu:

- 2 tbsp cocoa powder (unsweetened)
- 2 tbsp heavy whipping cream

- 2 tbsp whiskey
- ¼ cup espresso
- 3 ¼ cups mascarpone cheese
- 1 egg (separated)
- keto-friendly sweetener

Directions:

- Mix all of the cake ingredients in a bowl.
- Divide the batter into two mugs and microwave each mug for 90 seconds.
- Transfer the mug cakes to a plate to cool before slicing.
- Make a liquid for soaking by mixing the espresso, cream, and whiskey in a bowl. Soak the cake slices and set aside.
- In a separate bowl, whisk the egg white until you form stiff peaks.
- In another bowl, whisk the yolk and sweetener until it turns pale yellow in color.
- Add the mascarpone cheese and the soaking liquid then whisk well.
- Fold the egg white in.
- Assemble the mini tiramisu cakes in small dishes (or mugs). Start by placing the soaked cake slices at the bottom. Then top off with the tiramisu cream mixture.
- Before serving, dust the top with cocoa powder.

Brownie Cupcakes with Coconut Frosting

The richness of these cupcakes, combined with the creamy frosting makes for a perfect combination. Although simple, this recipe does require advanced preparation.

Time: 2 hours and 20 minutes

Serving Size: 8 cupcakes

Ingredients for the cupcakes:

- 1 tsp vanilla extract
- 2 tsp of baking powder
- 2 tbsp almond milk
- 3 tbsp coconut cream
- 6 tbsp coconut oil
- ⅓ cup walnuts (chopped)
- ½ cup cacao powder (unsweetened)
- ½ cup erythritol
- 1 cup almond flour

- 3 large eggs (whisked)
- a handful of walnuts (for garnish, chopped)

Ingredients for the frosting:

- 1 tsp vanilla extract
- 1 cup coconut cream
- erythritol

Directions:

- In a bowl, combine the coconut cream, vanilla extract, and a pinch of erythritol. Mix well using a wooden spoon.
- Set aside to cool and become semi-firm. Once semi-firm, transfer the frosting into a piping bag and place in the refrigerator to set completely.
- Preheat your oven to 350 °F and grease a cupcake pan.
- In a bowl, combine the vanilla extract, almond milk, coconut cream, and eggs then whisk well.
- In a separate bowl, combine the baking powder, cacao powder, erythritol, and almond powder then mix well. Stir the chopped walnuts in as well.
- Add coconut oil to the wet mixture and whisk well.
- Combine the wet mixture with the dry mixture and mix well to incorporate.
- Spoon the mixture into the muffin pan you have prepared.
- Place the muffin pan in the oven and bake the cupcakes for about 15 to 20 minutes.

- Take the muffin pan out of the oven and allow the cupcakes to cool completely.
- Once cooled, take the piping bag out of the oven and start frosting your cupcakes as desired. Then top off with chopped walnuts.

Chocolate Cupcakes with Avocado Buttercream Frosting

These cupcakes are the perfect dessert—and are perfect for any special occasion too. Topping them off with the buttercream frosting and you're sure to swoon in delight.

Time: 1 hour

Serving Size: 12 cupcakes

Ingredients for the cupcakes:

- 1 tsp vanilla extract
- 2 tsp of baking powder
- ¼ cup almond milk (unsweetened)
- ½ cup cacao powder
- ½ cup of coconut oil
- 1 cup erythritol (granulated)
- 2 cups almond flour
- 4 large eggs

Ingredients for the frosting:

- 1 tsp vanilla extract
- ¼ cup cacao powder
- 1 cup erythritol (powdered)
- 1 bar of chocolate (unsweetened, melted)
- 2 avocados (very ripe)

Directions:

- Preheat your oven to 175 °F and grease a cupcake pan.
- In a bowl, combine the dry cupcake ingredients and mix well.
- In a separate bowl, combine the wet cupcake ingredients and mix well.
- Add the wet ingredient mixture to the dry ingredient mixture and mix well.
- Spoon the batter into the cupcake pan you have prepared.
- Place the cupcake pan in the oven and bake the cupcakes for about 12 to 15 minutes.
- Take the cupcake pan out of the oven and allow to cool completely before adding the frosting.
- In a blender, add all of the frosting ingredients and blend until you get a smooth consistency.
- Pour the frosting into a piping bag and set aside until cupcakes have cooled completely. Once cool, add frosting to each of the cupcakes.

Key Lime Cupcakes

Key lime is the ultimate flavor for the summer season. But once you taste these cupcakes, you'll want to have them all year long!

Time: 40 minutes
Serving Size: 6 cupcakes

Ingredients for the cupcakes:

- ⅛ tsp of baking soda
- 2 tsp of baking powder
- 6 tbsp key lime juice (fresh)

- ⅓ cup coconut flour
- ⅓ cup coconut oil (melted)
- ½ cup of coconut sugar
- 3 large eggs
- sea salt

Ingredients for the frosting:

- 1 tbsp coconut sugar
- 1 tbsp key lime juice (fresh)
- 3 tbsp milk (non-dairy)
- ½ cup cashews (whole)
- key lime zest (from 4 key limes)

Directions:

- Preheat your oven to 350 °F and grease a cupcake pan.
- In a bowl, combine the key lime juice, coconut sugar, and eggs then beat well.
- In a separate bowl, combine the baking soda, baking powder, coconut flour, and a pinch of sea salt.
- Add the egg mixture and stir well to combine.
- Spoon the batter into the cupcake pan you have prepared.
- Place the cupcake pan in the oven and bake the cupcakes for about 20 to 25 minutes.
- Take the cupcake pan out of the oven and allow the cupcakes to cool down completely before adding the frosting.
- In a food processor, combine all of the frosting

ingredients. Pulse until you get a smooth consistency.

- Since cashew frosting doesn't have the same consistency as normal frosting, you would have to spread the frosting on the cupcakes using a butter knife. Then top off with some lemon zest for the final touch.

Red Velvet Cupcakes with Cream Cheese Frosting

Red velvet is a favorite flavor and for a good reason. In this keto-friendly cupcake form, these red velvet cupcakes are perfectly moist and tasty with rich cream cheese frosting.

Time: 50 minutes

Serving Size: 12 cupcakes

Ingredients for the cupcakes:

- ½ tsp keto-friendly sweetener (liquid)
- 1 tsp of baking soda
- 2 tsp of baking powder

- 2 tbsp cocoa powder (unsweetened)
- 2 tsp natural food coloring (red)
- 2 tsp vanilla extract
- 2 tsp white vinegar (distilled)
- 3 tbsp coconut flour
- ½ cup butter (melted)
- ½ cup erythritol
- 1 ½ cup almond flour
- 6 large eggs
- pink Himalayan salt

Ingredients for the frosting:

- ¼ tsp keto-friendly sweetener (liquid)
- 1 tsp vanilla extract
- 1 tbsp heavy cream
- ½ cup butter
- ½ cup erythritol (powdered)
- 1 cup cream cheese

Directions:

- Preheat your oven to 350 °F and grease a cupcake pan.
- In a bowl, combine the baking soda, baking powder, cocoa powder, coconut flour, erythritol, almond flour, and a pinch of pink Himalayan salt then whisk together well.
- In a separate bowl, combine the sweetener, food coloring, vanilla extract, butter, and eggs then mix well.
- Add the dry ingredient mixture and continue mixing to incorporate.

- Spoon the batter into the cupcake pan you have prepared.
- Place the cupcake pan in the oven and bake the cupcakes for about 20 to 25 minutes.
- Take the cupcake pan out of the oven and allow the cupcakes to cool down completely before adding the frosting.
- Use a hand mixer to beat the butter and cream cheese together using medium speed for about 3 to 4 minutes.
- Add the rest of the ingredients and continue beating until you get a fluffy texture.
- Once the cupcakes have cooled completely, you can either spread or pipe the frosting on each of the cupcakes.

Toasted Coconut Cupcakes

Love everything coconut? Then this dessert recipe is perfect for you. It's rich, buttery, and loaded with healthy fats and protein. Perfect for your keto diet!

Time: 20 minutes

Serving Size: 6 cupcakes

Ingredients for the cupcakes:

- ¼ tsp of baking powder
- 1 tsp vanilla extract
- 3 tbsp coconut sugar
- ¼ cup butter (melted)
- ¼ cup coconut flour
- ¼ cup coconut (unsweetened, shredded)
- 3 eggs
- salt

Ingredients for the topping:

- 2 tbsp coconut (unsweetened, shredded)

Directions:

- Preheat your oven to 400 °F and grease a cupcake pan.
- In a bowl, combine the vanilla extract, coconut sugar, butter, and eggs then whisk well to combine.
- Add the baking powder, coconut flour, coconut, and a pinch of salt and continue whisking to combine well.
- Spoon the batter into cupcake pan you have prepared then top each of the cupcakes with shredded coconut.
- Place the cupcake pan in the oven and bake the cupcakes for about 15 minutes.
- Take the cupcake pan out of the oven and allow them to cool down completely before serving.

Blueberry Muffins

Nothing says 'classic' like homemade blueberry muffins. If you're craving for a fruity pastry for your dessert, whip up a batch of these muffins and share it with those you love.

Time: 30 minutes

Serving Size: 12 muffins

Ingredients:

- ½ tsp vanilla extract
- 1 ½ tsp of baking powder
- ⅓ cup almond milk (unsweetened)
- ⅓ cup of coconut oil
- ½ cup erythritol (granulated)
- ¾ cup blueberries
- 2 ½ cup almond flour (blanched)
- 3 large eggs
- sea salt

Directions:

- Preheat your oven to 350 °F and grease a muffin pan.
- In a bowl, combine the baking powder, erythritol, almond flour, and a pinch of sea salt then mix well to combine.
- Add the vanilla extract, almond milk, coconut oil, and eggs then continue mixing.
- Gently fold the blueberries into the mixture.
- Spoon the batter into the muffin pan you have prepared.
- Place the muffin pan in the oven and bake the muffins for 20 to 25 minutes.
- Take the muffin pan out of the oven and allow the muffins to cool before serving.

Cinnamon Roll Muffins

Give the traditional cinnamon rolls a makeover by making them keto-friendly and in the form of muffins! These are super moist, sugar-free, but will satisfy your sweet tooth.

Time: 20 minutes
Serving Size: 20 muffins

Ingredients for the muffins:

- 1 tsp of baking powder
- 1 tbsp cinnamon
- ½ cup almond butter (or your choice of seed or nut butter)
- ½ cup almond flour
- ½ cup of coconut oil

- ½ cup pumpkin puree
- 2 scoops protein powder (vanilla)

Ingredients for the glaze:

- 2 tsp lemon juice (fresh)
- 1 tbsp keto-friendly sweetener (granulated)
- ¼ cup coconut butter
- ¼ cup milk

Directions:

- Preheat your oven to 350 °F and grease a muffin pan.
- In a bowl, combine all of the dry ingredients and mix thoroughly until well incorporated.
- Add the wet ingredients and continue mixing to combine well.
- Spoon the batter into the muffin pan you have prepared.
- Place the muffin pan in the oven and bake the muffins for about 10 to 15 minutes.
- Take the muffin pan out of the oven and allow the muffins to cool down for about 5 minutes before you transfer them to a wire rack.
- While waiting for the muffins to cool completely, prepare the cinnamon glaze. Combine all of the ingredients in a bowl and mix well.
- Drizzle the glaze over each of the muffins and allow to set before serving.

Coffee Cake Muffins

These tender muffins are moist, delicious, and are topped with cinnamon crumbs that add flavor and crunch. Enjoy them for dessert, breakfast, or any time of day.

Time: 50 minutes

Serving Size: 12 muffins

Ingredients for the topping:

- ¾ tsp cinnamon
- 2 tbsp coconut flour
- 3 tbsp keto-friendly sweetener
- ¼ cup butter (melted)
- ½ cup almond flour

Ingredients for the muffins:

- ½ tsp cinnamon
- ½ tsp vanilla extract
- 1 tbsp baking powder
- 3 tbsp coconut flour
- ¼ cup whey protein powder (unflavored)
- ⅓ cup keto-friendly sweetener
- ½ cup almond milk (unsweetened)
- ½ cup butter (melted)
- 2 cups almond flour
- 4 large eggs
- salt

Ingredients for the drizzle:

- ½ tsp vanilla extract
- 2 tbsp water
- ¼ cup keto-friendly sweetener (powdered)

Directions:

- In a bowl, combine all of the cinnamon, coconut flour, sweetener, and almond flour them mix well.
- Drizzle butter over mixture and continue mixing well to combine. Set aside.
- Preheat your oven to 325 °F and grease a muffin pan.
- In a bowl, combine the cinnamon, baking powder, coconut flour, sweetener, whey protein powder, almond flour, and a pinch of salt then mix well.

- Stir in vanilla extract, almond milk, butter, and eggs then continue mixing to combine well.
- Spoon the batter into the muffin pan you have prepared and top each of the muffins with the crumb topping.
- Place the muffin pan in the oven and bake the muffins for about 10 to 15 minutes.
- Take the muffin pan out of the oven and allow the muffins to cool down completely.
- In a bowl, combine all of the drizzle ingredients and mix well. After the muffins have cooled, drizzle lightly with the mixture.

Cranberry Orange Muffins

With their orange zest and fresh cranberries, these cupcakes are healthy, tasty, and of-so-perfect. As you bake them, the fragrance will surely put you in a festive mood.

Time: 50 minutes

Serving Size: 14 muffins

Ingredients:

- ½ tsp of baking soda
- 1 tsp vanilla bean (powdered)
- 1 tbsp orange zest
- ½ cup butter (grass-fed, unsalted)
- 1 cup cranberries (fresh, lightly crushed)
- 1 cup xylitol
- 1 ¼ coconut flour
- 8 eggs

- salt

Directions:

- Preheat your oven to 350 °F and grease a muffin pan.
- In a bowl, combine the baking soda, vanilla bean, orange zest, xylitol, coconut flour, and a pinch of salt then mix well.
- Add the butter and eggs to the mixture and combine thoroughly.
- Gently fold the cranberries into the mixture.
- Spoon the batter into the muffin pan you have prepared.
- Place the muffin pan in the oven and bake the muffins for about 25 to 35 minutes.
- Take the muffin pan out of the oven and serve the muffins warm.

Zucchini Muffins with Chocolate Chips

Zucchini and chocolate chips? This combination might make you raise your eyebrows. But once you've tasted the finished product, you'll definitely love this unique pairing.

Time: 45 minutes

Serving Size: 12 muffins

Ingredients:

- ½ tsp vanilla extract
- 2 tsp of baking powder
- ½ cup dark chocolate chips (sugar-free)
- ½ cup erythritol
- ⅔ cup ghee (melted)
- ¾ cup coconut flour
- 2 cups zucchini (grated or shredded)
- 6 large eggs
- sea salt

Directions:

- Preheat your oven to 350 °F and grease a muffin pan.
- In a bowl, combine the baking powder, erythritol, coconut flour, and a pinch of salt then mix well.
- Add the vanilla extract, zucchini, and eggs then continue mixing to combine well.
- Add the coconut oil and continue mixing to combine well.
- Fold the chocolate chips into the mixture and allow the batter to thicken for about 5 minutes.
- Spoon the batter into the muffin pan you have prepared. You may top each of the muffins with more chocolate chips if desired.
- Place the muffin pan in the oven and bake the muffins for about 35 minutes.
- Take the muffin pan out of the oven and allow the muffins to cool to room temperature. Then transfer the muffins to a wire rack and allow to cool completely.

CHAPTER 6:
Delicious Keto Ice Cream and Popsicle Recipes

THERE'S NOTHING LIKE cooling down after a satisfying meal with a bowl of ice cream—or a healthy popsicle. Even while following the ketogenic diet, you can still eat these sweet treats, especially when you make them on your own. Here, we will be going through some yummy ice cream and popsicle recipes to keep your diet fun, interesting, and sweet. Let's begin!

Butterscotch Ice Cream with Sea Salt

If you're craving a butterscotch-flavored treat with a hint of sea salt, here's a recipe to excite you. It's sweet, salty, and healthy all rolled into one!

Time: 10 minutes (freezing time not included)

Serving Size: 3 servings

Ingredients:

- ¼ tsp keto-friendly sweetener (liquid)
- ½ tsp xanthan gum
- 1 tsp sea salt (flaked)
- 2 tsp butterscotch flavoring

- 2 tbsp erythritol
- 2 tbsp vodka
- 3 tbsp butter (browned)
- 1 cup of coconut milk
- ¼ cup sour cream
- ¼ cup heavy whipping cream
- a handful of nuts (optional)

Directions:

- In a blender, combine all of the ingredients and blend well.
- Add the browned butter and nuts if desired.
- Transfer the mixture into a container with an airtight lid and place in the freezer for at least one hour (the longer, the better).

Choco Chunk Avocado Ice Cream

This ice cream is sweet, decadent, and has a lot of bitter chocolate chunks to make it a well-rounded dessert. The ingredients perfect the balance of this keto-friendly treat.

Time: 20 minutes (freezing time not included)

Serving Size: 6 servings

Ingredients:

- ¼ tsp keto-friendly sweetener (liquid)
- 2 tsp vanilla extract
- ½ cup of cocoa powder (unsweetened)

- ½ cup erythritol (powdered)
- ½ cup heavy whipping cream
- 1 cup of coconut milk
- 2 big avocados (Hass works best)
- 6 squares of baker's chocolate (unsweetened)

Directions:

- Cut avocados in half, remove the pits, and scoop out the flesh into an immersion blender.
- Add the vanilla extract, heavy cream, and coconut milk then blend until you get a creamy and smooth mixture.
- Add the sweetener, cocoa powder, and erythritol to the mixture then continue blending.
- Pour mixture into a bowl and set aside.
- Chop the baker's chocolate roughly, add into the mixture, and gently fold in with a spoon.
- Transfer the mixture into a container with an airtight lid and place in the freezer for about 6 to 12 hours before serving (the longer, the better).

Coffee Ice Cream

This coffee ice cream is creamy, rich, and low-carb too. Preparing it is a breeze, and the result is even better than what you can buy in stores!

Time: 15 minutes (freezing time not included)

Serving Size: 6 servings

Ingredients:

- ¼ tsp sea salt
- 1 ½ tsp cinnamon (ground)
- 4 tsp gelatin
- 1 tbsp vanilla extract
- ¼ cup instant coffee (granules)
- 1 cup keto-friendly sweetener
- 4 cups heavy whipping cream
- 3 eggs (yolks only)

Directions:

- In a saucepan, combine all of the ingredients and whisk well.
- Heat the saucepan on medium heat and continue to whisk until mixture starts giving off steam (but not boiling).
- Take the saucepan off the heat and allow the mixture to cool.
- Transfer the mixture into a container with an airtight lid and place in the freezer for at least four hours (the longer, the better).

Cookie Dough Ice Cream

This is another recipe that's a lot better than any store-bought ice cream out there. Since it's low-carb, you can enjoy this ice cream for your dessert or even as a cool snack!

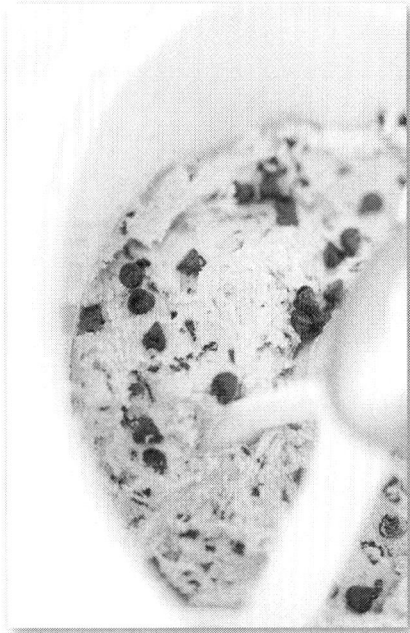

Time: 30 minutes (freezing time not included)
Serving Size: 6 servings

Ingredients for the vanilla ice cream:

- ¼ tsp sea salt
- 4 tsp gelatin
- 2 tbsp vanilla extract
- ½ cup keto-friendly sweetener

- 4 cups heavy whipping cream
- 3 eggs (yolks only)
- 1 vanilla bean (whole, scraped, optional)

Ingredients for the cookie dough:

- 3 tbsp coconut butter (melted)
- 3 tbsp maple-sweetened syrup (sugar-free)
- ¼ cup dark chocolate chips (sugar-free)
- 1 cup almond flour (finely ground)
- sea salt
- ½ tsp cinnamon (ground, optional)
- 1 tsp vanilla extract (optional)

Directions:

- Add all of the ice cream ingredients in a saucepan and whisk well.
- Heat the saucepan on medium heat and whisk constantly until the mixture starts giving off steam (but not boiling).
- Take the saucepan off the heat and allow the mixture to cool.
- Transfer the mixture into a container and place in the refrigerator to chill for at least one hour.
- In a bowl, combine all of the cookie dough ingredients and stir well. Do a taste test to see if you need to adjust the flavors.
- Roll the cookie dough into bite-sized balls, transfer to a freezer-safe container, and place in the freezer for at least one hour.
- Take the ice cream and cookie dough out of the refrigerator, combine, and mix well.

- Transfer the cookie dough ice cream into a container with an airtight lid and place in the freezer for at least two hours (the longer, the better).

Creamy Coconut Ice Cream

There's something irresistible about the subtle creamy sweetness of this ice cream. It has a very strong coconut flavor that will surely keep you coming back for more.

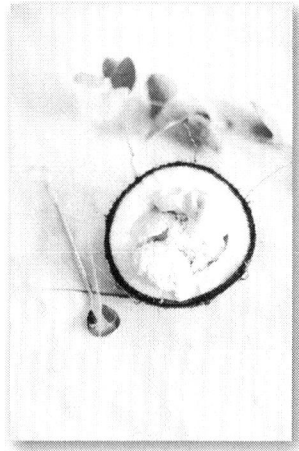

Time: 30 minutes (freezing time not included)
Serving Size: 8 servings

Ingredients:

- 5 tbsp erythritol
- 1 ½ cups coconut flakes
- 1 ¾ cups coconut milk (full-fat)
- 3 ¼ cups coconut cream

Directions:

- In a pan, toast the coconut flakes. Take off the heat, set aside, and allow to cool completely.

- In a bowl, add the coconut milk and coconut cream then stir well.
- Add the sweetener, and toasted coconut then stir well.
- Transfer the mixture into a container with an airtight lid and place in the freezer for at least two hours (the longer, the better).

Lemon Curd Ice Cream

This keto-friendly ice cream it tangy, healthy, and delicious. It has the great flavor of lemon sans the carbs. It's creamy, dreamy, and always hits the spot!

Time: 45 minutes (freezing time not included)
Serving Size: 10 servings

Ingredients:

- 2 tsp lemon zest (grated)
- 4 tbsp butter
- ¼ cup lemon juice (fresh)
- ⅓ cup keto-friendly sweetener (powdered)
- ½ cup keto-friendly sweetener (powdered, for the lemon curd)
- 1 ½ cup heavy whipping cream
- 3 large eggs
- 2 tbsp vodka (optional)

Directions:

- In a bowl set over a pan filled with water that's simmering gently, combine the lemon zest, lemon juice, sweetener, and eggs then whisk continuously for 10 minutes to thicken.
- Once it thickens, remove the bowl from the heat and add the butter.
- Set aside for a couple of minutes, allowing the butter to melt then resume whisking until creamy and smooth.
- Add the whipping cream and sweetener then continue whisking until well combined. If you want to use vodka, whisk it in as well.
- Transfer the mixture into a container with an airtight lid and place in the freezer for at least three hours (the longer, the better).

Mixed Berry Ice Cream

This is one of the easiest recipes out there as you can finish it in a matter of 5 minutes. Plus it's full of berry goodness with a texture that's rich, creamy, and healthy too.

Time: 5 minutes (freezing time not included)
Serving Size: 2 servings

Ingredients:

- ¼ tsp keto-friendly sweetener
- ½ tsp vanilla extract
- 5 tbsp heavy whipping cream (grass-fed)
- 1 ½ cups mixed berries (frozen)
- sea salt

Directions:

- In a blender, combine all of the ingredients and process until you get a smooth consistency.
- Transfer the mixture into a container with an airtight lid and place in the freezer for at least two hours (the longer, the better).

Mocha Ice Cream

This is another smooth and creamy ice cream recipe that requires very few ingredients. It's the perfect summer treat, the perfect dessert, and it's just... perfect!

Time: 10 minutes (freezing time not included)

Serving Size: 4 servings

Ingredients:

- 1 tsp vanilla extract
- 2 cups brewed coffee (strong)
- 2 cups heavy cream
- ½ cup of cocoa powder
- ½ cup keto-friendly sweetener

Directions:

- In a pan, heat the brewed coffee, heavy cream, cocoa powder, and sweetener on medium heat.
- After the ingredients are mixed well, add the vanilla extract.

- Pour the mixture in a bowl and allow to cool down completely.
- Once cool, transfer the mixture into a container with an airtight lid and place in the freezer for at least three hours (the longer, the better).

Pumpkin Pie Ice Cream with Pecans

The flavors and textures in this ice cream work really well together. After the initial bite of creamy pumpkin, you will be able to savor the flavors of pecan and maple. Yum!

Time: 20 minutes (freezing time not included)

Serving Size: 4 servings

Ingredients:

- ⅕ tsp keto-friendly sweetener (liquid)
- ½ tsp xanthan gum

- 1 tsp maple extract
- 1 tsp pumpkin spice
- 2 tbsp butter (salted)
- ⅓ cup erythritol
- ½ cup cottage cheese
- ½ cup pecans (toasted, chopped)
- ½ cup pumpkin purée
- 2 cups of coconut milk (unsweetened)
- 3 big eggs (yolks only)

Directions:

- In a pan, heat the butter and toasted pecans on low heat until the butter browns. Then take the pan off the heat and set aside.
- In an immersion blender, add the remaining ingredients then blend until you get a smooth mixture.
- Add the butter and pecans then continue blending until just incorporated.
- Transfer the mixture into a container with an airtight lid and place in the freezer for at least two hours (the longer, the better).

Vanilla Bean Ice Cream

Going back to the classics, you'll soon discover that this keto-friendly ice cream is really amazing! It's easy to make, super quick to bring together, and oh-so-yummy.

Time: 50 minutes (freezing time not included)

Serving Size: 12 servings

Ingredients:

- ¼ tsp xanthan gum
- 1 tsp vanilla extract
- ¾ cup erythritol
- 1 cup almond milk (vanilla, unsweetened)
- 3 cups heavy whipping cream
- 1 vanilla bean (halved, scraped, seeds reserved)
- 2 large eggs
- sea salt

Directions:

- In a bowl, combine the xanthan gum, erythritol, and the seeds of the vanilla bean, mix well, and set aside.
- In a separate bowl, add the eggs and beat with a whisk. Add the erythritol mixture gradually as you continue to whisk.
- Add the vanilla extract, almond milk, heavy cream, and a pinch of salt. Mix well until evenly incorporated.
- Transfer the mixture into a container with an airtight lid and place in the freezer for at least three hours (the longer, the better).

Blueberry Lemonade Popsicles

These popsicles are cool, refreshing, and tasty too! Whether you eat these popsicles for dessert or as a light snack on a hot day, they will always hit the spot.

Time: 5 minutes (freezing time not included)

Serving Size: 6 popsicles

Ingredients:

- ½ tsp keto-friendly sweetener (liquid)
- 2 tsp coconut oil
- ¼ cup heavy cream
- ¼ cup sour cream
- ⅔ cup blueberries (rinsed)
- 1 cup of coconut milk
- ½ lemon (juiced)

Directions:

- In a blender, combine all of the ingredients and blend for 30 seconds on high.
- Carefully pour mixture into your popsicle mold. Place a stick in each of the molds then set with the cover.
- Place in the freezer for at least 4 hours.

Fat Bomb Popsicles

Fat bombs are very popular on the keto diet because they're tasty and they help you reach your daily fat requirement. Here's a recipe for fat bombs—but in popsicle form.

Time: 15 minutes (freezing time not included)

Serving Size: 6 popsicles

Ingredients:

- 1 tbsp keto-friendly sweetener
- 1 tbsp vanilla extract
- ½ cup raspberries (organic)
- 1 cup blueberries (organic)
- 3 cups coconut cream (divided)

Directions:

- Fill the bottom of your popsicle molds individually with a few blueberries.
- In a food processor combine the sweetener,

vanilla extract, and 2 cups of coconut cream then process until you get a smooth consistency.

- Pour mixture into molds about ¼-inch over the blueberries at the bottom then set the mixture aside.

- Place a stick into each of the molds and place the popsicle mold into the freezer for about 1 hour until almost solid.

- In a food processor, combine the raspberries with 1 cup of coconut cream then process until you create a smooth mixture.

- Pour ½-inch of the mixture into each of the molds then return the popsicle mold to the freezer for 1 hour.

- Repeat these steps by alternating between the blueberry and raspberry mixtures until you've filled the individual molds to the top.

- Once full, return the popsicle mold to the freezer for at least 4 hours.

Key Lime Popsicles

These popsicles have a gorgeous color that makes them look refreshing. Once you bite into them, you'll discover that they're just sweet enough to make you feel satisfied.

Time: 5 minutes (freezing time not included)

Serving Size: 10 popsicles

Ingredients:

- ½ tsp vanilla extract
- ⅓ cup keto-friendly sweetener
- ½ cup lime juice (fresh)
- 2 cups of coconut milk (full-fat)
- 2 cups macadamia nut milk (unsweetened)
- sea salt
- 3 drops food coloring (green, optional)

Directions:

- In a blender, combine all of the ingredients and blend until everything is well incorporated.
- Carefully pour mixture into your popsicle mold. Place a stick in each of the molds then set with the cover.
- Place in the freezer for at least 4 hours.

Strawberry Cream Popsicles

These delightful popsicles are low-carb, creamy, and refreshingly delicious. Enjoy them after your meals or any time you feel like having a sweet treat!

Time: 10 minutes (freezing time not included)

Serving Size: 8 popsicles

Ingredients:

- ¼ tsp xanthan gum
- 1 tsp strawberry extract (or vanilla extract)
- ⅓ cup keto-friendly sweetener
- 1 cup almond milk (unsweetened)
- 1 cup heavy cream
- 1 cup strawberries (fresh, mashed)

Directions:

- In a saucepan, heat the sweetener, almond milk, heavy cream, and strawberries on medium heat. Whisk until you get a smooth consistency.
- Bring the mixture to a boil. Then turn the heat

down, allowing the mixture to simmer for a few minutes until it thickens slightly.

- Take the saucepan off the heat and add the strawberry extract. Continue whisking the mixture as you add xanthan gum.

- Transfer the mixture to an immersion blender and blend everything together well. Just be careful when blending the hot mixture as it might cause your blender to explode—you may want to pause once in a while and take off the lid.

- Once fully incorporated, set the mixture aside to cool down completely.

- Once cool, carefully pour mixture into your popsicle mold. Place a stick in each of the molds then set with the cover.

- Place in the freezer for at least 4 hours.

Turmeric Popsicles

These creamy popsicles get their lovely color from the natural tint of the main ingredient—turmeric. They also have a pleasantly unique bite that might surprise you.

Time: 5 minutes (freezing time not included)
Serving Size: 4 popsicles

Ingredients:

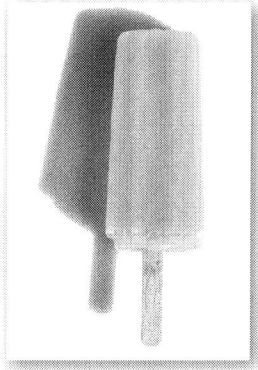

- 1 tsp ginger (ground)
- ½ tbsp turmeric powder
- 1 cup of coconut milk
- a pinch of black pepper
- erythritol

Directions:

- In a small pot, heat the coconut milk and add the spices and sweetener. Mix until everything is well incorporated.
- Carefully pour mixture into your popsicle mold. Place a stick in each of the molds then set with the cover.
- Place in the freezer for at least 4 hours.

CHAPTER 7:
Delicious Keto Pudding and Mousse Recipes

NEXT UP, WE have some delicious pudding and mousse recipes that will fit right into your ketogenic diet. The great thing about pudding and mousse is that they have a wonderful texture that feels indulgent and satisfying. Of course, these recipes have been modified to be suitable for the keto diet—which means that you can enjoy them without feeling guilty about deviating from your ketogenic journey. Read on to learn how to make luscious puddings and mousses!

Almond Joy Chia Pudding

This first dessert is healthy, delicious, and comes together quickly. It has a creamy texture with a crunchy topping that makes it extremely addictive and fun to eat.

Time: 1 hour and 20 minutes

Serving Size: 4 servings

Ingredients:

- 1 tsp vanilla extract
- 2 tbsp almonds (roasted, crushed)
- ¼ cup of cocoa powder (unsweetened)
- ¼ cup erythritol (powdered)
- ⅓ cup chia seeds
- ½ cup coconut flakes (unsweetened, divided)
- 2 cups almond milk (unsweetened)
- ¼ cup dark chocolate chips (unsweetened, optional)

Directions:

- In a blender, combine the vanilla extract, cocoa powder, erythritol, almond milk, and half of the coconut milk then blend to combine well.
- Transfer the mixture into a bowl, add the chia seeds, the vigorously whisk for two minutes.
- Pour the pudding mixture into 4 serving cups or bowls and place in the refrigerator for a minimum of 1 hour.
- Before serving, top with almonds, coconut flakes, and chocolate chips (if desired).

Banana Pudding

This dessert is so tasty that you might not believe it's low-carb! It contains all the good things banana pudding must have sans the excess sugar and artificial ingredients.

Time: 2 hours and 35 minutes

Serving Size: 12 servings

Ingredients for the layer of cookie:

- 1 tsp of baking powder
- 1 tsp vanilla extract
- 2 tbsp butter (softened)
- ¼ cup erythritol (confectioner›s variety)
- ½ cup almond flour (superfine)
- 1 egg

Ingredients for the layer of pudding:

- 2 tsp vanilla extract
- ½ cup erythritol (confectioner›s variety)

- 1 cup almond milk (unsweetened)
- 2 cups heavy whipping cream
- 1 medium-sized banana (sliced very thinly)
- 6 eggs (yolks only)

Ingredients for the layer of whipped cream:

- ¼ tsp xanthan gum
- 1 tsp vanilla extract
- ¼ cup erythritol (confectioner›s variety)
- ½ cup heavy whipping cream

Directions:

- Preheat your oven to 350 °F and use parchment paper to line a baking sheet.
- In a bowl, combine the vanilla, butter, and egg then blend using an electric mixer.
- Add the baking powder, erythritol, and almond flour then continue mixing until well incorporated.
- Pour mixture into the baking sheet and spread into an even layer.
- Place the baking sheet in the oven and bake the cookie layer for about 12 to 15 minutes.
- Take the baking sheet out of the oven and allow the cookie sheet to cool.
- In a bowl, add the egg yolks and set aside.
- In a saucepan, heat the vanilla extract, erythritol, almond milk, and heavy cream on medium heat while stirring frequently.
- When steam starts coming out of the mixture, take the saucepan off the heat.

- Gradually pour some of the mixture into the bowl with the egg yolks while whisking until you get a smooth, uniform texture.
- Then gradually pour the egg yolk mixture back into the cream mixture while whisking.
- Place the saucepan back on the stove—this time on medium-low heat—to cook the mixture while stirring constantly.
- As the mixture thickens, try to observe then it's thick enough to coat the back part of a spoon. When this happens, take the saucepan off the heat and set it aside to cool slightly.
- As the pudding mixture cools down, cut the cookie layer into 1-inch cubes.
- In a pudding dish, pour half of the pudding mixture and spread evenly. Top with half of the cookie cubes to form another layer. Add another layer using half of the banana slices.
- Repeat these steps by adding layers of pudding, cookies, and banana slices.
- Cover the dish loosely then place in the refrigerator for about 2 hours.
- Before serving, make the whipped cream. Use an electric mixer to combine all of the whipped cream ingredients. Whip until you form stiff peaks then spread the whipped cream over the banana pudding.

Coconut Pudding

Are you looking for a traditional low-carb, keto-friendly pudding recipe? If so, you'll enjoy this creamy pudding that's made with cream cheese, coconut milk, and more.

Time: 15 minutes

Serving Size: 4 servings

Ingredients:

- ½ tsp vanilla extract
- 1 tsp coconut extract
- ¼ cup keto-friendly sweetener (granulated)
- ½ cup coconut (unsweetened, shredded)
- ½ cup cream cheese (cut into small pieces)
- ½ cup coconut cream
- ½ cup of coconut milk
- 1 egg (beaten)

Directions:

- In a microwave-safe bowl, combine vanilla extract, coconut extract, sweetener, and half of the coconut cream.
- Microwave the ingredients on high for 1 minute and let stand.
- In a bowl, combine the egg with the remaining coconut cream, beat well, and set aside.
- In a saucepan, add the cream cheese and coconut milk. Cook the ingredients on medium heat to melt the cream cheese.
- Add the mixture you heated in the microwave and continue cooking to heat the mixture through.
- Add the beaten mixture and continue stirring until you form a thick pudding mixture.
- Pour the pudding mixture into baking dishes, allow to cool and place in the refrigerator to chill.

Coffee Custard Pudding

Love coffee? Then you'll have fun making—and eating—this dish. It's a low-carb pudding that's high in fat to ensure that you stay in ketosis even after having dessert!

Time: 20 minutes

Serving Size: 4 servings

Ingredients:

- ¼ tsp cream of tartar
- ¾ tsp keto-friendly sweetener (liquid)
- 1 tsp espresso powder (instant)
- ¼ cup butter (unsalted)
- ½ cup mascarpone cheese
- 4 large eggs (separated)

Directions:

- In a saucepan, combine the butter and mascarpone cheese. Cook on low heat until melted.
- Add the egg yolks and espresso powder while whisking.
- Continue cooking while occasionally stirring until mixture thickens.
- Take the saucepan off the heat, add the sweetener, and mix to incorporate.
- In a bowl, combine the cream of tartar with the egg whites and beat until you form stiff peaks.
- Fold the egg white mixture into the custard mixture gently to form the pudding.
- Spoon the pudding into serving bowls and place in the refrigerator to chill.

Key Lime and Avocado Pudding

This pudding is so tasty that it just might become your new favorite. It's a decadent, creamy pudding with a nutty topping—the perfect combination!

Time: 15 minutes

Serving Size: 2 servings

Ingredients for the pudding:

- ½ tsp vanilla extract
- 1 tsp key lime zest
- 2 tbsp coconut milk (full-fat)
- 2 tbsp key lime juice
- 2 tbsp maple syrup
- 2 medium-sized avocado (ripe)

Ingredients for the topping:

- ¼ tsp cinnamon (powdered)
- 1 tsp coconut oil
- 1 tsp maple syrup
- 2 tbsp almond flour (blanched)
- 2 tbsp walnuts (chopped)

Directions:

- Preheat your oven to 300 °F and grease a baking sheet.
- In a blender, combine all of the pudding ingredients and blend until you get a creamy and smooth consistency.
- Pour the pudding into 2 serving bowls and place in the refrigerator to chill.
- Combine all of the topping ingredients on greased baking dish and spread out evenly.
- Place the baking dish in the oven, and bake the topping for about 10 minutes. Halfway through the baking time, take out the baking dish and stir the ingredients.
- Take the baking dish out of the oven and allow to cool for 5 minutes.
- Before serving the pudding, top off with the crumbled topping.

Pistachio Pudding

This tasty pudding will bring back your childhood memories. It's luscious, rich, and it doesn't even involve any cooking. Here's how to make his healthy dessert.

Time: 20 minutes

Serving Size: 6 servings

Ingredients:

- ½ tsp vanilla extract
- 2 tbsp erythritol (confectioner's variety)
- 3 tbsp pistachios (chopped)
- 1 cup mascarpone cheese
- 1 ½ almond milk (unsweetened)
- 1 ½ cups heavy whipping cream
- 2 packs pistachio pudding mix (sugar-free)

Directions:

- In a bowl, combine the almond milk, pudding mix, and ½ cup of whipping cream.
- Mix everything together well then place the bowl in the refrigerator to chill for about 15 minutes.
- In a separate bowl, combine the vanilla extract, erythritol, and the rest of the heavy cream. Use an electric mixer to whisk until you form stiff peaks.
- Fold in half of the cream mixture into the chilled pistachio mixture gently.
- Once fully incorporated, spoon the pudding into 6 serving dishes.
- Spoon the remaining cream mixture over the top and sprinkle with chopped pistachios.

Cappuccino Cheesecake Mousse

This low-carb mousse is made with healthy ingredients making it suitable for your new diet. But when you taste it, you'll be surprised at how creamy and rich it is.

Time: 15 minutes

Serving Size: 8 servings

Ingredients:

- ½ tsp vanilla extract
- 2 tsp coffee extract
- ¼ cup brewed coffee (strong)
- ½ cup almond milk (unsweetened)
- 1 cup heavy whipping cream
- 2 cups cream cheese (softened)
- coffee beans (optional)

Directions:

- In a stand mixer, combine the coffee and cream cheese then blend until you get a smooth consistency.
- Add the vanilla extract, almond milk, and half of the coffee extract. Continue blending to incorporate, then set aside.
- In a separate bowl, add the heavy cream and whip until you form stiff peaks.
- Fold in the whipped cream into the mixer and resume blending to combine well.
- Spoon the mousse mixture into 8 serving dishes then place in the refrigerator to chill.
- Before serving, top with coffee beans if desired.

Chocolate Mousse

Who says you can't enjoy chocolate mousse while on keto? This decadent dessert will prove them wrong. It's simple, easy to make, and doesn't require chilling!

Time: 10 minutes

Serving Size: 4 servings

Ingredients:

- ¼ tsp kosher salt
- 1 tsp vanilla extract
- ¼ cup of cocoa powder (unsweetened, sifted)
- ¼ cup keto-friendly sweetener (powdered)
- 1 cup heavy whipping cream

Directions:

- In a bowl, whisk the heavy cream until you form stiff peaks.
- Add the rest of the ingredients and continue whisking until well incorporated.
- Spoon the mousse into 4 serving dishes and serve!

Coconut and Strawberry Mousse

If you're always craving for a sweet bite after your meals, then this delectable dessert is another great option. It has a wonderful flavor that will satisfy your taste buds.

Time: 5 minutes

Serving Size: 2 servings

Ingredients:

- 1 tbsp keto-friendly sweetener (confectioner's variety)
- 2 tbsp coconut (unsweetened, shredded)
- 2 tbsp heavy cream
- ½ cup coconut cream (unsweetened, full-fat)
- ½ cup mascarpone cheese
- ½ cup strawberries (diced)

Directions:

- One day before making this mousse, place the coconut milk in the refrigerator overnight to separate the cream from the water. The cream—which is creamy and thick—is what you need for the recipe.

- In a food processor, combine all of the ingredients then process until you get a creamy and smooth consistency.
- Spoon the mousse into 2 serving dishes, sprinkle with shredded coconut, and top with a fresh strawberry.

Lemon Cheesecake Mousse

This sweet mousse also comes with a fresh lemon flavor making it extremely pleasant to the taste. It's also an excellent way to add more healthy fats into your diet as a dessert.

Time: 8 minutes

Serving Size: 6 servings

Ingredients:

- ⅓ cup keto-friendly sweetener (confectioner's variety)
- ⅔ cup lemon curd (same as the one used for "Lemon Curd Ice Cream")
- 1 cup cream cheese
- 1 cup heavy cream (cold)

Directions:

- In a bowl, add the heavy cream then whip until you form soft peaks.
- In a separate bowl, add the cream cheese then use a hand mixer to whip.
- Add the sweetener, and lemon curd then continue whipping.

- Add the whipped cream and continue whipping to combine well.
- Spoon the mousse into 6 serving dishes and place in the refrigerator to chill for at least 10 minutes.

Mascarpone Cheese Mousse with Strawberries

This tasty mousse is smooth, sweet, and topped off with freshly roasted strawberries. Elegant as it looks, it's a simple dessert to make.

Time: 40 minutes

Serving Size: 6 servings

Ingredients for the strawberries:

- ¼ tsp vanilla extract
- 2 tsp keto-friendly sweetener (granulated)
- 2 cups strawberries (quartered)

Ingredients for the mousse:

- 1 tsp vanilla extract
- 6 tbsp keto-friendly sweetener (powdered, divided)
- ½ cup cream cheese (softened)
- 1 cup mascarpone cheese (softened)
- 1 cup whipping cream

Directions:

- Preheat your oven to 375 °F and grease a baking sheet lightly.
- Add strawberries to the baking dish, spread out, and sprinkle with the sweetener.
- Add the vanilla extract then toss lightly to combine.
- Place the baking sheet in the oven and roast the strawberries for about 20 to 25 minutes.
- Take the baking sheet out of the oven and allow the roasted strawberries to cool.
- In a bowl, combine the vanilla extract, cream cheese, mascarpone cheese, and 4 tablespoons of the sweetener then mix well to combine.
- In a separate bowl, combine the whipping cream with the rest of the sweetener then whip until you form stiff peaks.
- Gently fold the whipped cream into the cheese mixture and combine well.
- Spoon the mousse into 6 serving dishes and top with the roasted strawberries.

Peanut Butter Mousse

This recipe is just as simple as the others, but it will surely be one of the most popular you make. It has a salty-sweet flavor that's oh-so-addictive!

Time: 5 minutes

Serving Size: 4 servings

Ingredients:

- ½ tsp vanilla extract
- ¼ cup peanut butter (natural, sugar-free)
- ¼ cup keto-friendly sweetener (powdered)
- ½ cup cream cheese (softened)
- ½ cup heavy whipping cream
- chocolate sauce (low-carb, optional)

Directions:

- In a bowl, add the whipping cream, whip until you form stiff peaks, and set aside.
- In a separate bowl, combine the peanut butter

and cream cheese then beat until you get a creamy and smooth mixture.

- Add the vanilla extract and sweetener then continue beating until smooth.
- Gently fold the whipped cream into the mixture until well combined.
- Spoon the mousse into 4 serving dishes and drizzle with chocolate sauce if desired.

Raspberry Mousse

This is another recipe that is ridiculously easy and uncomplicated. It's effortless, guilt-free, and delightful with its refreshingly vibrant flavors.

Time: 10 minutes

Serving Size: 3 servings

Ingredients:

- ½ tbsp raspberry gelatin (sugar-free)
- 1 ¼ cups raspberry yogurt (sugar-free)
- 2 cups whipped topping (sugar-free)
- mint (fresh)
- raspberries (fresh)

Directions:

- In a bowl, combine gelatin and yogurt then whisk well until both ingredients are well incorporated.
- Separate 3 tablespoons of the whipped topping and set aside.

- Gently fold the rest of the whipped topping into the bowl until well combined.
- Spoon the mousse into 3 serving dishes and place in the refrigerator for about 2 hours to set.
- Before serving, top with 1 tablespoon of whipped cream, fresh raspberries, and mint leaves.

CHAPTER 8:
Delicious Keto Sweet Bread and Loaf Recipes

WE'RE NOT DONE yet! Now let's go through some heavier keto-friendly recipes. You can enjoy these different types of sweet bread and loaves for dessert, for breakfast or even as a light snack when you're feeling hungry in between meals. Although the recipes aren't as easy as the other recipes we have already gone through, they're still fairly simple and easy to follow. Also, these recipes are so interesting and delicious that the extra time and effort you put into making them is worth the effort.

Blueberry Bread

This low-carb bread is chock-full of blueberries giving it a rich flavor. It's grain-free, sugar-free, gluten-free, and perfect for keto dieters like you!

Time: 1 hour

Serving Size: 1 bread loaf

Ingredients:

- 1 tsp vanilla extract
- 1 ½ tsp of baking powder
- 2 tbsp coconut flour
- 3 tbsp butter (softened)
- 3 tbsp heavy whipping cream
- ½ cup blueberries
- ½ cup erythritol
- 2 cups almond flour
- 5 eggs

Directions:

- Preheat your oven to 350 °F and line a loaf pan with parchment paper.
- In a bowl, combine the vanilla extract, sweetener, and egg then use a mixer to combine for 3 minutes until the eggs turn frothy.
- Add the heavy cream and continue mixing for 2 more minutes.
- In a bowl, combine the baking powder, coconut flour, erythritol, and almond flour then mix well. Add the butter then continue mixing to combine everything together.
- Add the frothy mixture and mix until well incorporated.
- Fold the blueberries in then pour batter into the loaf pan.
- Place the loaf pan in the oven and bake the bread for about 45 to 50 minutes.
- Take the loaf pan out of the oven and allow to cool before slicing.

Cinnamon Swirl Bread

Here's another tasty dessert which you can eat for breakfast too. After baking, you can enjoy this bread on its own or toast a few slices with butter to make them richer.

Time: 45 minutes

Serving Size: 1 bread loaf

Ingredients:

- ¼ tsp cream of tartar
- ¼ tsp keto-friendly sweetener (liquid)
- 1 tsp of baking powder
- 1 tsp vanilla extract
- 1 ½ tsp cinnamon (divided)
- 4 tbsp butter (2 tbsp melted, 2 tbsp softened)

- ¼ cup erythritol (confectioner›s variety)
- ¾ cup cream cheese (softened)
- 1 cup almond flour
- 4 eggs (separated)

Directions:

- Preheat your oven to 350 °F and line a loaf pan with parchment paper.
- In the bowl with the egg whites, add the cream of tartar, use an electric mixer to beat until you form soft peaks, and set aside.
- In the bowl with the egg yolks, add sweetener, vanilla extract, softened butter, and cream cheese then mix well to combine.
- Add the baking powder, almond flour, and ½ teaspoon of cinnamon then continue mixing to combine well.
- In a separate bowl, combine the erythritol, melted butter, and the remaining cinnamon, stir well, and set aside.
- Fold the egg white mixture into the egg yolk mixture until well combined.
- Pour half of the batter into the loaf pan and top with the cinnamon mixture.
- Add the rest of the batter and spread evenly.
- Use a knife to create swirls in between the layers of batter. Don't move the knife around too much so as not to mix the layers.
- Place the loaf pan into the oven and bake the bread for about 30 to 40 minutes.
- Take the load pan out of the oven and allow the bread to cool down before slicing.

Cream Cheese Bread

As with the other bread recipes we have here, you can enjoy this one without feeling guilty about breaking your diet. It's a light and airy bread that's low in sugar and carbs.

Time: 35 minutes

Serving Size: 1 bread loaf

Ingredients:

- 1 tsp keto-friendly sweetener
- 1 tsp sea salt
- 4 tsp of baking powder
- ½ cup butter (unsalted)
- ½ cup sour cream (full-fat)
- 1 cup cream cheese (full-fat)
- 1 ½ cups coconut flour
- 1 egg (for the egg wash)
- 8 large eggs
- 2 tbsp sesame seeds (optional)

Directions:

- Preheat your oven to 350 °F and line a loaf pan with parchment paper.
- In a bowl, combine the sweetener, sea salt, baking powder, and coconut flour then mix well.
- In a separate bowl, combine the butter and cream cheese then use an electric mixer on medium speed to beat the ingredients together until you get a fluffy and light consistency.
- Add eggs one by one while you continue mixing.
- Turn down the speed of the mixer to low as you gradually add the dry ingredient mixture and continue mixing until fully incorporated.
- Gently fold the sour cream into the mixture and incorporate well.
- Pour batter into the loaf pan until it's slightly overfilled.
- In a bowl, beat the egg for the egg wash. Brush the top of the batter with egg wash and sprinkle with sesame seeds if desired.
- Place the loaf pan in the oven and bake the bread for about 90 minutes.
- Take the loaf pan out of the oven and allow the bread to cool before slicing.

Gorilla Bread

This recipe brings the classic monkey bread to a whole new level as it's filled with cream cheese. This is one of the most indulgent desserts you can make for yourself.

Time: 1 hour and 15 minutes

Serving Size: 24 bread balls

Ingredients for the topping:

- 1 tsp butter
- 2 tsp cinnamon
- ½ cup keto-friendly sweetener
- ½ cup pecans (optional)

Ingredients for the bread:

- 1 tsp vanilla extract
- 2 tsp of baking powder
- 1 tbsp butter
- 1 tbsp keto-friendly sweetener

- ¼ cup coconut flour
- ¼ cup cream cheese
- ½ cup almond flour
- 1 cup mozzarella cheese
- 1 egg

Ingredients for the filling:

- 2 tbsp butter (melted)
- 1 cup cream cheese

Directions:

- Preheat your oven to 350 °F and grease a pie plate with butter.
- In a bowl, combine the sweetener, cinnamon, and butter then mix well. Sprinkle 1 teaspoon of this mixture all over the pie plate then set aside. Also, sprinkle pecans if desired.
- In a microwave-safe bowl, combine the mozzarella and cream cheese then microwave for 1 minute. Stir then microwave for 30 seconds. Stir again then microwave for 30 more seconds.
- In a food processor, combine the melted cheese with the remaining bread ingredients. Process until you get a dough with a uniform color.
- Transfer the dough on a sheet of parchment paper then cut into 24 pieces.
- Cut the cream cheese into the same number of pieces. Sprinkle each piece of dough with ¼ teaspoon of cinnamon sweetener, place a cube of cream cheese in the middle, and roll into a ball.

- Dip the ball of dough in butter, coat with the cinnamon sweetener, and place in the pie plate you have prepared. Repeat these steps with all the pieces of dough.
- Place the pie plate in the oven and bake the gorilla bread for about 45 to 50 minutes.
- Take the pie plate out of the oven, allow the gorilla bread to cool down for 10 minutes, then invert the pan onto a plate before serving.

Hawaiian Sweet Bread

Hawaiian sweet bread is so good which is why it's part of this dessert recipe book. This popular bread is keto-friendly and comes loaded with all the right flavors.

Time: 30 minutes

Serving Size: 10 pieces of sweet bread

Ingredients:

- ⅛ tsp pineapple oil
- 1 tsp ginger paste (fresh)
- 2 tsp of baking powder
- ½ cup cream cheese
- ¾ cup keto-friendly sweetener (powdered)
- 1 ½ cups almond flour
- 3 cups mozzarella cheese (shredded)
- 2 eggs

Directions:

- In a bowl, combine the baking powder, sweetener, and almond flour then mix well.
- In a microwave-safe bowl, combine the cream cheese and mozzarella cheese and melt on high for about 1 ½ minutes.
- For the next steps, you have to work fast!
- Add the melted cheese to the dry ingredient mixture and mix well to combine.
- Add pineapple oil, ginger paste, and eggs then continue mixing to combine well.
- Transfer the dough to a sheet of parchment paper then knead the dough until bubbles start forming.
- Cut the dough into 10 pieces and roll each piece into a ball.
- Grease a baking pan and place all of the dough balls on it.
- Place the baking pan in the oven and bake the sweet bread at 425 °F for about 15 to 20 minutes.
- Take the baking pan out of the oven and allow the sweet bread to cool before removing from the pan.

Spiced Sweet Bread

You can enjoy this spiced sweet bread for dessert at any time of the year. The great thing about this recipe is that you can customize the ingredients according to your liking.

Time: 35 minutes

Serving Size: 1 bread loaf

Ingredients:

- ¼ tsp cardamom (ground)
- ¼ tsp cloves (ground)
- ¼ tsp white pepper
- ½ tsp nutmeg (ground)
- 1 tsp cinnamon
- 1 tsp vanilla extract
- 1 tsp xanthan gum
- 1 ½ tsp of baking powder
- 1 tbsp cacao nibs
- 2 tbsp cacao powder (unsweetened)

- 2 tbsp psyllium powder
- ⅓ cup cacao butter (melted)
- ⅓ cup MCT oil
- ½ cup dark chocolate (sugar-free, roughly chopped)
- ½ cup flax meal
- ½ cup keto-friendly sweetener
- ¾ cup almond meal
- 6 eggs
- ½ cup hazelnuts (chopped, optional)

Directions:

- Preheat your oven to 350 °F and grease a loaf pan with butter.
- In a bowl, combine all of the ingredients and mix well.
- Gently scoop the batter into the loaf pan you have prepared. Use a wet spatula to smoothen the top. Sprinkle with chopped hazelnuts if desired.
- Place the loaf pan in the oven and bake the bread for about 50 minutes.
- Take the loaf pan out of the oven and allow the bread to cool down for about one hour before slicing.

Banana Loaf

This low-carb banana loaf is rich, moist, and the perfect addition to your diet. It stores well, and it's really versatile too. Here are the steps for making this recipe...

Time: 1 hour and 10 minutes

Serving Size: 1 loaf

Ingredients:

- 2 tsp of baking powder
- 2 tsp banana extract
- 2 tsp cinnamon
- 6 tbsp butter (softened)
- ¼ cup almond milk (unsweetened)
- ¼ cup coconut flour
- ½ cup erythritol
- ½ cup walnuts (chopped)
- 2 cups almond flour (blanched)
- 4 big eggs
- ¼ tsp sea salt (optional)

Directions:

- Preheat your oven to 350 °F and use parchment paper to line a loaf pan.
- In a bowl, combine the baking powder, cinnamon, coconut flour, almond flour, and a pinch of salt if desired, then mix well to combine.
- In a separate bowl, combine the erythritol and butter then beat until fluffy with a hand mixer. Add the eggs as you continue beating, followed by the almond milk and banana extract.
- Continue beating as you add the dry ingredient mixture.
- Stir the walnuts in and mix to incorporate.
- Pour batter into the loaf pan you have prepared and use a spatula to smoothen the top. You may top off with more walnuts if desired.
- Place the loaf pan in the oven and bake the loaf for about 50 to 60 minutes.
- Take the loaf pan out of the oven and allow the loaf to cool down before slicing.

Double Chocolate Zucchini Loaf

This moist loaf is almost cake-like, making it very appealing as a dessert. It's also a fun way to incorporate more veggies into your diet while enjoying every sweet bite.

Time: 1 hour and 5 minutes

Serving Size: 1 loaf

Ingredients:

- ¼ tsp salt
- ½ tsp cinnamon (ground)
- 1 tsp of baking powder
- 1 tsp of baking soda
- 1 tsp vanilla extract
- ¼ cup of coconut oil
- ½ cup of chocolate chips (sugar-free)
- ½ cup of cocoa powder (unsweetened)
- ½ cup coconut flour
- ½ cup keto-friendly sweetener (powdered)

- 2 cups zucchini (shredded)
- 4 large eggs

Directions:

- Preheat your oven to 350 °F and use parchment paper to line a loaf pan.
- In a bowl, combine salt, cinnamon, baking powder, baking soda, cocoa powder, coconut flour, sweetener then mix well.
- Add the vanilla extract, coconut oil, and eggs then continue mixing until well incorporated.
- Fold in the chocolate chips and zucchini.
- Pour batter into loaf pan you have prepared.
- Place the loaf pan in the oven and bake the loaf for about 45 to 55 minutes.
- Take the loaf pan out of the oven and allow the loaf to cool down completely before slicing.

Egg Loaf with Lemon and Blueberries

This unique loaf will soon be one of your favorite keto desserts. The lemon adds some zing to the flavor while the blueberries provide the sweetness. Perfect!

Time: 35 minutes

Serving Size: 1 loaf

Ingredients:

- ¼ tsp nutmeg
- 1 tsp of baking powder
- 1 tsp vanilla extract
- 2 tbsp butter
- 3 tbsp keto-friendly sweetener
- ½ cup blueberries
- 1 cup cream cheese
- 2 lemons (zest only)
- 8 large eggs
- maple syrup (sugar-free, for drizzling)

Directions:

- Preheat your oven to 350 °F and use parchment paper to line a bundt pan.
- In a blender, combine all of the ingredients except for the blueberries then blend until you get a smooth consistency.
- Pour batter into the bundt pan you have prepared then sprinkle in all of the blueberries around the pan.
- Place the bundt pan in the oven and bake the loaf for about 30 to 40 minutes.
- Take the bundt pan out of the oven, allow the loaf to cool for about 5 minutes, then flip it out onto a serving plate while warm. Drizzle with maple syrup before serving.

Cranberry Loaf

Who says you can only eat cranberries during thanksgiving? As long as you bake this bread, you can enjoy cranberries as your dessert any time you want!

Time: 1 hour and 10 minutes

Serving Size: 1 loaf

Ingredients:

- 1 tsp salt
- ½ tsp of baking soda
- 1 ½ tsp of baking powder
- 3 tbsp butter (softened)
- ¾ cup of orange juice
- 1 cup keto-friendly sweetener
- 1 ½ cups cranberries (chopped)
- 2 cups flour
- 1 egg
- 1 tsp orange zest (optional)
- ¾ cup nuts (chopped, optional)
- 1 cup raisins (optional)

Directions:

- Preheat your oven to 350 °F and use parchment paper to line a loaf pan.
- In a bowl, combine salt, baking powder, baking soda, sweetener, and flour then mix well.
- Add the butter, orange juice, and egg then continue mixing. Also, add the orange zest if desired.
- Fold the cranberries in along with any additional nuts or fruit if desired.
- Pour batter into the pan you have prepared.
- Place the loaf pan in the oven and bake the loaf for about 55 to 60 minutes.
- Take the loaf pan out of the oven and allow the loaf to cool down before slicing.

Gingerbread Loaf

This keto-friendly gingerbread loaf is perfectly seasoned with nutmeg, ginger, and cinnamon. It has that classic flavor you love sans the carbs and sugar.

Time: 1 hour

Serving Size: 1 loaf

Ingredients:

- ¼ tsp of baking soda
- ¼ tsp salt
- ½ tsp nutmeg (ground)
- 1 tsp of baking powder
- 1 tsp dark molasses
- 2 tsp cinnamon
- 3 tsp ginger (ground)
- ¼ cup coconut flour

- ¼ cup coffee (brewed)
- ½ cup butter (softened)
- ½ cup maple syrup (sugar-free)
- 1 cup almond flour
- 2 eggs

Directions:

- Preheat your oven to 320 °F and use parchment paper to line a loaf pan.
- In a bowl, combine the baking soda, salt, nutmeg, baking powder, cinnamon, ginger, coconut flour, and almond flour then mix well.
- In a microwave-safe bowl, combine butter, dark molasses, and syrup then melt in the microwave for about 45 seconds.
- Allow the heated mixture to cool for a while. Once cool, add the eggs and mix well.
- Add the liquid mixture to the dry ingredient mixture and add the coffee too. Mix well together.
- Pour batter into the loaf pan you have prepared.
- Place the pan in the oven and bake the loaf for about 50 minutes.
- Take out of the oven and allow the loaf to cool down completely before slicing.

Pumpkin Loaf with Cream Cheese

This delicious low-carb loaf has a creamy and sweet filling that's absolutely lovely. It's extremely moist, and it contains a combination of spices that work perfectly together.

Time: 1 hour and 10 minutes

Serving Size: 1 loaf

Ingredients:

- ¼ tsp vanilla extract
- ½ tsp cinnamon (ground)
- ½ tsp cloves (ground)
- ½ tsp pumpkin pie spice
- ½ tsp salt
- ¾ tsp vanilla extract
- 1 tsp orange extract
- 1 ½ tsp of baking powder
- 1 tbsp coconut flour
- ¼ cup erythritol (powdered)
- ½ cup of coconut oil

- ¾ cup erythritol (confectioner's variety)
- 1 cup cream cheese
- 1 cup pumpkin purée
- 1 ⅔ cups almond flour
- 1 egg
- 5 eggs

Directions:

- Preheat your oven to 325 °F and use parchment paper to line a loaf pan.
- In a bowl, combine the ¼ tsp vanilla extract, ¼ cup erythritol (powdered), coconut flour, orange extract, cream cheese, and 1 egg then beat until you get a smooth texture, and set aside.
- In a separate bowl, combine the cinnamon, cloves, pumpkin pie spice, salt, and almond flour, mix well, and set aside.
- In another bowl, combine the ¾ tsp vanilla extract, ¾ cup erythritol (confectioner's variety), coconut oil, pumpkin purée, and 5 eggs then beat well.
- Add the flour mixture and continue beating until just combined.
- Pour ½ of the batter into the loaf pan you have prepared.
- Spoon the cream cheese mixture on top then pour the other half of the batter over it.
- Place the pan in the oven and bake for about 50 to 60 minutes.
- Take the pan out of the oven and allow to cool down before slicing.

CHAPTER 9:
Delicious Keto Dessert Pizza, Bars, and Crepe Recipes

IF YOU LOVE pizza, you'd be happy to know that this particular food item doesn't always have to be savory. These days, pizzas can be anything you want them to be—even a dessert! This chapter is all about sweet pizzas as well as bars and crepes. You can make all of these in your own kitchen with just a few ingredients. The more recipes you learn, the more you build your dessert knowledge, enrich of your diet, and make it more fun all around. Let's get baking!

Chocolate Cookie Pizza

This is an easy dessert pizza with a delectable chocolate crust. It's basically a giant cookie with cream cheese frosting and fruits—or any other sweet topping you want.

Time: 1 hour

Serving Size: 1 pizza

Ingredients for the crust:

- ¼ tsp salt
- ½ tsp vanilla extract
- 1 tsp of baking powder
- 2 tbsp butter (melted)
- ⅓ cup of cocoa powder
- ⅓ cup keto-friendly sweetener (granulated)
- 1 ¾ cups almond flour
- 1 egg

Ingredients for the frosting:

- ½ tsp vanilla extract

- 2 tbsp heavy cream
- ¼ cup keto-friendly sweetener (powdered)
- ½ cup cream cheese

Ingredients for the topping:

- ⅛ cup of chocolate chips (sugar-free)
- ¼ cup blueberries
- ¼ cup heavy whipping cream
- 5 big strawberries (sliced)

Directions:

- Preheat your oven to 300 °F and use parchment paper to line a round baking sheet. Also, line your work surface with another sheet of parchment paper.
- In a bowl, combine salt, baking powder, cocoa powder, sweetener, and almond flour then whisk well to combine.
- Add the vanilla extract, butter, and egg then continue mixing until you form a dough.
- Transfer the dough onto your work surface and pat into a circular shape.
- Place another sheet of parchment paper on top of the dough ball and roll out into a circle. Crimp and press the edges of the circle to make it even.
- Slide the dough onto the baking sheet you have prepared, place the baking sheet in the oven, and bake the pizza crust for 30 minutes.
- Take the baking sheet out of the oven and set aside to cool.

- In a bowl, combine the sweetener and cream cheese then beat until you get a smooth consistency.
- Add the vanilla extract and heavy cream then continue beating until well-combined.
- After the crust has cooled down, generously spread the frosting all over it.
- Arrange the blueberries and strawberries decoratively on top of your pizza.
- In a microwave-safe bowl, add the cream and microwave for 30 seconds.
- Add the chocolate chips and let stand for about 2 minutes to melt. Once melted, whisk together well to make a sauce.
- Drizzle the sauce over your cookie pizza then place in the refrigerator to chill for about 20 minutes before serving.

Fruit Pizza

If you're craving a sweet and fresh dessert pizza, whip this up in your kitchen right away! It's tasty, healthy, and super-easy to put together.

Time: 40 minutes

Serving Size: 1 pizza

Ingredients for the crust:

- 1 tsp vanilla extract
- 4 tbsp butter (unsalted, softened)
- ¼ cup cream cheese (softened)
- ⅓ cup erythritol (granulated)
- 1 cup almond flour (superfine)
- 1 large egg

Ingredients for the frosting:

- 1 tsp vanilla extract
- 2 tbsp butter (unsalted, softened)
- ¼ cup cream cheese (softened)
- ¼ cup erythritol (confectioner›s variety)
- ½ cup heavy whipping cream

Ingredients for the topping:

- ¾ cup blueberries (washed)
- 1 cup strawberries (washed, quartered)

Directions:

- Preheat your oven to 300 °F and use parchment paper to line a round baking sheet.
- In a bowl, combine the vanilla extract, butter, cream cheese, and erythritol then use an electric mixer to combine well.
- Add the egg and continue mixing until well incorporated.
- Add the almond flour and mix until you get a creamy and smooth batter.
- Use a rubber spatula to transfer the batter onto the baking sheet you have prepared. Top it off with another sheet of parchment then roll out the crust into a circular shape.
- Remove the sheet of parchment from the top of the crust, place the baking sheet in the oven, and bake the crust for about 20 to 25 minutes.
- Take the baking sheet out of the oven and allow the crust to cool down completely.
- In a bowl, combine the vanilla extract, butter, cream cheese, and erythritol then use an electric mixer blend everything together well.
- Add the heavy cream, turn your mixer on high, and continue mixing until the mixture has doubled in size.
- After the crust has cooled down completely, spread generously with frosting. Then top the pizza off with the fruits before serving.

Cream Cheese Pizza with Fruits

This is another simple pizza recipe that you can share with the rest of the family. This time, you would use a ready-made crust—unless you want to make it from scratch.

Time: 25 minutes

Serving Size: 1 pizza

Ingredients:

- 1 tsp vanilla extract
- ¼ cup blueberries
- ¼ cup keto-friendly sweetener (powdered)
- ½ cup strawberries (sliced)
- ½ cup whipping cream
- 1 cup cream cheese
- 1 cauliflower dessert crust (frozen)

Directions:

- Preheat your oven to 375 °F and use parchment paper to line a round baking sheet. Bake the dessert crust according to the directions on the label.
- Take the baking sheet out of the oven and allow the crust to cool down completely.
- In a bowl, combine the sweetener and cream cheese then use an electric mixer to beat until fluffy.
- Add the vanilla extract and whipping cream then continue beating until smooth.
- Once the crust has cooled down completely, spread the cream cheese mixture over it, and top with berries.

Strawberry Limeade Pizza

This dessert pizza is refreshing and comes with a sweet cookie crust made mainly from almond flour. It's the perfect dessert for summer cookouts and dinners.

Time: 15 minutes

Serving Size: 1 pizza

Ingredients for the crust:

- 1 tsp vanilla extract
- 2 tbsp keto-friendly sweetener
- 8 tbsp butter
- 1 ½ cup almond flour

Ingredients for the frosting:

- 1 tsp vanilla extract
- 2 tbsp almond milk
- 2 tbsp heavy cream
- ¼ cup keto-friendly sweetener
- ¾ cup cream cheese

- 1 lime (grated zest, juiced)

Ingredients for the topping:

- 1 cup strawberries (sliced thinly)

Directions:

- Preheat your oven to 350 °F and use parchment paper to line a round baking sheet.
- In a bowl, combine the vanilla extract, sweetener, butter, and almond flour then mix well until you form a soft dough.
- Transfer the dough to the baking sheet you have prepared and roll it out evenly.
- Place the baking sheet in the oven and bake the crust for about 6 to 7 minutes.
- Take the baking sheet out of the oven and allow the crust to cool down completely.
- In a blender, combine all of the frosting ingredients and blend until fully incorporated.
- Once the crust has cooled completely, spread frosting, and top with the sliced strawberries.
- Place the pizza in the refrigerator to chill before serving.

Sugar Cookie Pizza with Fruits and Nuts

Sugar cookies make the best crust for keto-friendly pizzas. Even non-keto dieters would love to eat this pizza for dessert. It's sugar-free and easy to make too.

Time: 20 minutes

Serving Size: 1 pizza

Ingredients for the crust:

- 1 tsp salt
- 1 tsp vanilla extract
- 1 tsp xanthan gum
- 6 tbsp butter (cold, diced)
- ¼ cup keto-friendly sweetener
- 1 ¾ cup almond flour
- 1 egg (beaten)

Ingredients for the frosting:

- ½ tsp vanilla extract
- ¼ cup keto-friendly sweetener

- ¼ cup sour cream
- ¾ cup cream cheese (softened)

Ingredients for the topping:

- ¼ cup blueberries
- ½ cup blackberries
- ½ cup raspberries
- ½ cup strawberries (sliced)

Directions:

- In a food processor, combine salt, vanilla extract, xanthan gum, sweetener, and almond flour then pulse together.
- Add the butter and continue pulsing until you get a crumbly mixture.
- Add the egg and continue pulsing until you form a dough.
- Form the dough into a ball, wrap with plastic, and chill in the refrigerator for 1 hour.
- In a bowl, combine the frosting ingredients and whisk together until you get a fluffy and smooth mixture.
- Place the bowl in the refrigerator until ready to spread.
- After 1 hour of chilling the dough, take it out of the refrigerator and roll it into a circle shape.
- Preheat your oven to 375 °F and use parchment paper to line a round baking sheet.
- Place the crust on baking sheet, place the baking sheet in the oven, and bake the crust for about 10 to 12 minutes.

- Take the baking sheet out of the oven and allow the crust to cool down completely.
- Once cool, take the frosting out of the oven, and spread it all over the crust.
- Top off with the fresh berries and place back in the refrigerator to chill before serving.

Caramelized Pecan Pie Bars

These are rich, low-carb dessert bars with an extremely satisfying buttery crust. As you eat them, you won't even notice that they're entirely egg and sugar-free.

Time: 55 minutes

Serving Size: 16 bars

Ingredients for the crust:

- 2 tbsp butter (salted, melted)
- ⅓ cup keto-friendly sweetener (confectioner's variety)
- ⅓ cup whey protein powder
- 1 cup coconut (shredded)
- 2 cups almond flour

Ingredients for the sauce:

- ⅛ tsp salt
- ½ tsp vanilla extract
- 1 tbsp brandy

- 4 tbsp butter (salted)
- ¼ cup keto-friendly sweetener
- ⅓ cup maple syrup
- ¾ cup heavy cream
- 2 ½ cups pecans

Directions:

- Preheat your oven to 350 °F and use parchment paper to line a baking sheet.
- Spread the pecans all over the baking sheet, place the baking sheet in the oven, and toast the pecans for about 8 to 12 minutes.
- Take the baking sheet out of the oven, allow the pecans to cool down completely, and chop roughly.
- Grease another baking sheet and line with a sheet of parchment paper.
- In a saucepan, combine the butter, maple syrup, and heavy cream then heat on medium heat while stirring constantly.
- Bring to a boil, turn the heat down to low, and allow the mixture to cook for about 20 more minutes to thicken while stirring occasionally.
- Take the caramel sauce off the heat, add the rest of the ingredients, and mix until well incorporated.
- In a bowl, combine all of the dry crust ingredients and whisk together thoroughly.
- Add the butter and continue mixing until fully incorporated.
- Pour batter onto a baking sheet you have prepared then set aside.

- Combine the caramel sauce with the pecans and mix well together. Pour this mixture over the crust and use a spatula to spread it evenly.
- Place the baking sheet in the oven and bake the pecan pie bars for about 25 minutes.
- Take the baking sheet out of the oven and allow the pecan pie bars to cool down completely before slicing into squares.

Coconut Cheesecake Bars

These dessert bars are for cheesecake lovers and coconut lovers alike. They're light, fluffy, and you might discover that you can't just eat one piece at a time!

Time: 1 hour and 40 minutes
Serving Size: 12 bars

Ingredients for the base:

- ¼ tsp salt
- 3 tbsp erythritol
- 5 tbsp butter (unsalted, melted)
- ¼ cup coconut flour
- 1 ¼ cups almond flour

Ingredients for the cheesecake:

- ½ tsp salt
- 1 tbsp vanilla extract
- ½ cup heavy whipping cream
- ¾ cup erythritol
- 1 cup coconut cream

- 2 cups cream cheese (softened)
- 3 eggs

Directions:

- Preheat your oven to 350 °F and use parchment paper to line a baking sheet.
- In a bowl, combine all of the base ingredients together and mix well until you get a crumbly consistency.
- Transfer the mixture to the baking sheet, press down, and smoothen evenly.
- Place the baking sheet in the oven and bake the crust for about 15 to 20 minutes.
- Take the baking sheet out of the oven, allow the crust to cool down, and chill in the refrigerator.
- In a bowl, use an electric mixer to beat the cream cheese until you get a fluffy and smooth mixture.
- Add the erythritol and continue beating until smooth.
- Add eggs one by one as you continue beating to ensure that the texture remains smooth.
- Add the salt, coconut cream, heavy cream, and vanilla extract then whisk until you get a smooth consistency.
- Pour the mixture over the chilled crust.
- Place the baking sheet into a bigger baking pan filled with hot water. The water should come up to two-thirds of the baking sheet.
- Place the baking pan and baking sheet into the oven and bake for about 1 hour and 20 minutes to make the cheesecake firm.

- Open the door of your oven slightly allowing the dessert bars to cool slightly.
- Once cool, place the baking sheet in the refrigerator and allow the dessert bars to chill overnight before slicing into squares.

Matcha Fudge Bars

These aren't just dessert bars—they're fat bombs too! Whip up these fudgy matcha bars for dessert tonight, but try not to snack on too many of these regularly!

Time: 20 minutes
Serving Size: 15 bars
Ingredients:

- ¼ tsp keto-friendly sweetener (powdered)
- 1 tbsp cranberries (dried, sugar-free, chopped)
- 1 tbsp matcha powder
- 1 tbsp pistachios (chopped)
- 2 tbsp coconut butter
- ½ cup cacao butter
- ½ cup cashew butter
- ½ cup coconut cream

Directions:

- In a pot, bring water to a boil. Then lower the heat and allow to simmer.
- Place a heat-proof bowl over the pot, add

the cacao butter, and continuously stir until melted.

- Once melted, take the bowl off the heat and add the sweetener, matcha, coconut butter, cashew butter, and coconut cream then mix well until you get a creamy and smooth consistency.
- Use a sheet of parchment paper to line a baking pan and pour the mixture in it.
- Sprinkle with matcha powder and top with cranberries and pistachios.
- Place the baking pan in the refrigerator and chill for at least 4 hours before serving.

Samoa Bars

When you have these Samoa bars to enjoy after your meals, you won't be craving for other high-sugar desserts anymore. And the best part is—they're so easy to make!

Time: 45 minutes

Serving Size: 16 bars

Ingredients for the crust:

- ¼ tsp salt
- ¼ cup butter (melted)
- ¼ cup keto-friendly sweetener
- 1 ¼ cups almond flour

Ingredients for the chocolate filling:

- 2 tbsp coconut oil
- ½ cup dark chocolate (sugar-free, chopped)

Ingredients for the caramel filling:

- ¼ tsp salt

- ½ tsp vanilla extract
- 3 tbsp butter
- ½ cup keto-friendly sweetener
- ¾ cup heavy whipping cream
- 1 ½ cups coconut (shredded)

Directions:

- Preheat your oven to 325 °F and use parchment paper to line a baking sheet.
- In a bowl, combine salt, sweetener, and almond flour then whisk well.
- Add the butter and continue mixing until well incorporated.
- Transfer the mixture into the baking sheet you have prepared and press it down firmly.
- Place the baking sheet in the oven and bake the crust for 15 to 18 minutes.
- Take the baking sheet out of the oven and allow the crust to cool down.
- In a microwave-safe bowl, combine coconut oil and chocolate. Heat the ingredients in 30-second increments until they are melted, smooth, and well incorporated.
- Spread ⅔ of the chocolate sauce over the crust.
- In a skillet, heat the coconut on medium heat, toast while stirring constantly, and set aside.
- In a saucepan, combine the butter and sweetener on medium heat and bring to a boil. Boil until golden for about 4 minutes.
- Take the saucepan off the heat and add the salt, vanilla extract, and heavy cream.

- Add the toasted coconut and mix well to incorporate.
- Pour mixture over the cooled crust and spread evenly.
- Allow cooling before cutting the bars into squares.
- Reheat the remaining chocolate sauce and drizzle over the Samoa bars.

S'mores Bars

This classic campfire snack gets a gluten-free, low-carb makeover with this recipe. These dessert bars will bring back your favorite childhood treat in a healthier way.

Time: 1 hour and 5 minutes

Serving Size: 16 bars

Ingredients for the crust:

- ¼ tsp salt
- ½ tsp cinnamon
- ½ tsp vanilla extract
- 5 tbsp butter (chilled, cut into pieces)
- ¼ cup keto-friendly sweetener (granulated)
- 1 ½ cups almond flour

Ingredients for the filling:

- ½ cup dark chocolate (sugar-free, chopped)
- ¾ cup whipping cream

Ingredients for the topping:

- ¼ tsp cream of tartar
- ½ tsp vanilla extract
- 3 tbsp keto-friendly sweetener (granulated)
- 3 tbsp keto-friendly sweetener (powdered)
- 3 large eggs (whites only)
- salt

Directions:

- Preheat your oven to 325 °F and use parchment paper to line a baking pan.
- In a food processor, combine salt, cinnamon, vanilla extract, sweetener, and almond flour then pulse to combine.
- Sprinkle in the pieces of butter as you continue pulsing until you get a crumbly mixture.
- Transfer the mixture to the baking pan you have prepared and press down firmly.
- Place the baking pan in the oven and bake for about 12 to 15 minutes.
- Take the baking pan out of the oven and allow the crust to cool down.
- In a saucepan, add the cream and bring to a simmer.
- Add the chocolate and leave for about 5 minutes to melt.
- Once melted, whisk gently until smooth.
- Pour mixture over the crust then place the baking pan in the refrigerator for 1 hour until firm.
- Turn down the heat of your oven to 300 °F.

- In a bowl, combine the cream of tartar with egg whites, and a pinch of salt then beat until frothy.
- Continue beating as you add the vanilla extract and sweeteners until you form stiff peaks.
- Spread the mixture over the chilled crust and filling, place the baking pan in the oven, and bake for about 20 minutes.
- Take the baking pan out of the oven, allow the dessert bars to cool, then place in the refrigerator for at least 1 hour to set before cutting into squares.

Blueberries and Cream Crepes

When it comes to crepes, blueberries and cream are a classic. Crepes are a heavier kind of dessert that you can pair with a light meal. Dig into these sweet crepes!

Time: 30 minutes

Serving Size: 2 crepes

Ingredients for the crepes:

- ⅛ tsp keto-friendly sweetener
- ⅛ tsp sea salt
- ¼ tsp of baking soda
- ¼ tsp cinnamon
- ¼ cup cream cheese
- 2 big eggs

Ingredients for the filling:

- ½ tsp vanilla extract
- 2 tbsp erythritol
- ½ cup blueberries
- ½ cup cream cheese

Directions:

- In a bowl, combine the eggs, and cream cheese then use an electric hand mixer to beat until smooth.
- Add the sea salt, baking soda, cinnamon, and sweetener then continue mixing to combine well.
- Heat a non-stick pan on medium heat and grease lightly with butter.
- Pour the crepe batter—about ¼ cup each time—then swirl the pan to spread the mixture all the way to the edges of the pan.
- Cook the crepes for about 3 minutes until the edges are crispy. Once cooked, transfer to a plate.
- In a bowl, combine the vanilla extract, erythritol, and cream cheese then use an electric mixer to beat until you get a creamy and smooth consistency.
- Assemble your crepes. Start with a crepe, add the filling down the middle, top with fresh blueberries, and fold accordingly. Top off with a dash of cinnamon if desired.

Choco-Hazelnut Crepes

This is a unique crepe recipe that gives you a different texture for the crepes. Of course, these crepes are still tasty, and learning how to make them gives you a different option.

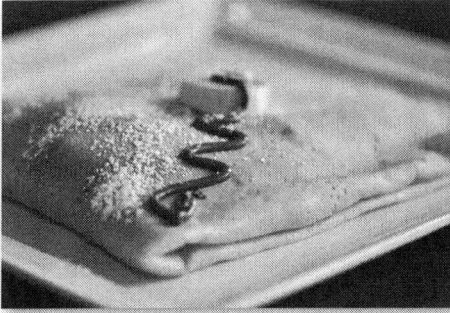

Time: 20 minutes

Serving Size: 3 crepes

Ingredients:

- ½ tsp vanilla extract
- 2 tbsp keto-friendly sweetener
- ¼ cup cream cheese
- ¼ cup Nutella spread (same as the one used for «Cake Roll with Nutella»)
- ¼ cup of water
- ½ cup almond flour
- 3 eggs

Directions:

- In a microwave-safe bowl, add the cream cheese then microwave for about 20 seconds. Stir until you get a creamy and smooth consistency.
- Add the eggs and mix well to combine.
- Add the vanilla extract, sweetener, and almond flour then continue mixing until well incorporated.
- Add water and whisk well.
- Heat a non-stick pan on low heat and grease lightly with butter.
- Pour the crepe batter—about ¼ cup each time—then swirl the pan to spread the batter all the way to the edges of the pan.
- Cook the crepes for about 3 minutes until the edges are crispy. Once cooked, transfer to a plate.
- Fill with homemade Nutella, fold accordingly, and serve.

Cream Cheese Crepes

These low-carb crepes contain a special ingredient that makes them unique. They also have a buttery flavor that goes well with savory or sweet fillings.

Time: 15 minutes

Serving Size: 4 crepes

Ingredients:

- ¼ cup mascarpone cheese
- 2 large eggs
- filling of your choice
- ½ tsp cinnamon (optional for sweet crepes)
- ½ tsp vanilla extract (optional for sweet crepes)
- 1 tsp erythritol (optional for sweet crepes)
- sea salt (optional for savory crepes)

Directions:

- In a blender, combine all of the ingredients and blend until you get a smooth batter.

- Heat a non-stick pan on low heat and grease lightly with butter.
- Pour the crepe batter—about ¼ cup each time—then swirl the pan to spread the mixture to the edges of the pan.
- Cook the crepes for about 3 minutes until the edges are crispy. Once cooked, transfer to a plate.
- Add the filling of your choice, fold accordingly, and serve.

Raspberries and Cream Crepes

Have these healthy crepes for dessert or as a light breakfast to start your day. The filling of these crepes will surely warm you up and make you feel satisfied.

Time: 15 minutes

Serving Size: 5 crepes

Ingredients for the crepes:

- 2 tbsp erythritol
- ¼ cup cream cheese
- 2 eggs
- cinnamon
- salt

Ingredients for the filling and topping:

- ⅓ cup raspberries (fresh)
- ½ cup whole ricotta cheese
- maple syrup (sugar-free, optional)
- whipped cream (optional)

Directions:

- In a blender, combine the erythritol, cream cheese, eggs, a dash of cinnamon, and a pinch of salt then blend until you get a smooth batter.
- Heat a non-stick pan on low heat and grease lightly with butter.
- Pour the crepe batter—about ¼ cup each time—then swirl the pan to spread the batter to the edges of the pan.
- Cook the crepes for about 3 minutes until the edges are crispy. Once cooked, transfer to a plate.
- Spread ricotta cheese on each of the crepes, add a few raspberries and fold accordingly. Top with whipped cream and a drizzle of maple syrup if desired.

Snickerdoodle Crepes

Snickerdoodles are always a treat, and this time, they come in the form of crepes. This recipe is so good that your whole family will surely love it just as much as you!

Time: 10 minutes

Serving Size: 4 servings

Ingredients for the crepes:

- 1 tsp cinnamon
- 1 tbsp keto-friendly sweetener (granulated)
- ⅔ cup cream cheese (softened)
- 6 eggs

Ingredients for the filling:

- 2 tbsp cinnamon
- 8 tbsp butter (softened)
- ⅓ cup keto-friendly sweetener (granulated)

Directions:

- In a blender, combine all of the crepe ingredients then blend for 5 minutes.
- Heat a non-stick pan on low heat and grease lightly with butter.
- Pour the crepe batter—about ¼ cup each time—then swirl the pan to spread the batter all the way to the edges of the pan.
- Cook the crepes for about 3 minutes until the edges are crispy. Once cooked, transfer to a plate.
- In a bowl, combine the cinnamon and sweetener then mix well.
- Add half of the mixture into the butter and mix until smooth.
- Spread butter mixture onto the middle of each crepe, fold accordingly and sprinkle with cinnamon sweetener mixture before serving.

CHAPTER 10:
Delicious Keto Sweet Snack Recipes

FOR THIS FINAL chapter of recipes, let's change things up by focusing on sweet snacks instead of desserts—although you can always enjoy these for a light dessert too! No matter what diet you're on, snacking always seems to be an important aspect of it. If you love snacks, then you might as well ensure that the snacks you eat will satisfy you and won't cause you to break your diet—even if you're craving for a sweet snack. To help you out with this, here are some sweet and healthy snack recipes you can easily make at home!

Almond Butter Cups

Are you ready for a sweet, delectable, and simple recipe? These almond butter cups are easy to make and require a few ingredients only. Read on!

Time: 25 minutes
Serving Size: 12 butter cups

Ingredients:

- 1 tbsp coconut oil
- 1 tbsp erythritol (granulated)
- 1 ½ tbsp coconut flour
- ¼ cup almond butter
- ¼ cup chocolate (extra dark)

Directions:

- In a bowl, combine the erythritol, coconut flour, and almond butter, mix until well combined, and set aside.
- In a microwave-safe bowl, combine coconut oil and chocolate, melt, and mix until smooth.

- Spoon the melted chocolate into parchment cups then swirl it around to cover the bottom completely and about ⅓ of the sides.
- Spoon the almond butter mixture into the center of each parchment cup then cover with chocolate completely.
- Place the parchment cups in the freezer until the butter cups solidify.

Birthday Cake Shake

Have you ever heard of a birthday cake shake? This is a tasty treat that comes with all the goodness of birthday cake in the form of a drink. And it's so easy to make!

Time: 5 minutes

Serving Size: 2 servings

Ingredients:

- ⅛ tsp almond extract
- ¼ tsp vanilla extract
- 1 tbsp butter (grass-fed, softened)
- ¼ cup heavy cream
- ⅓ cup whey protein powder (vanilla)
- 1 cup almond milk (vanilla, unsweetened)
- 1 cup ice (crushed)
- sprinkles
- whipped cream
- xanthan gum (optional)

Directions:

- In a blender, add the heavy cream and blend for 1 to 2 minutes until the cream has thickened.
- Add the almond extract, vanilla extract, butter, and almond milk then continue blending for 30 seconds.
- Add the protein powder and ice then continue blending for 1 to 2 minutes more.
- Add a pinch of xanthan gum if desired for sweetness and thickness. Continue blending for a few more seconds.
- Pour into two glasses then top off with sugar-free whipped cream and sprinkles.

Blueberry Cheesecake Squares

Make the most of blueberry season with these sweet squares. They're low-carb, healthy, and serve as a filling snack. This recipe is another easy one for you.

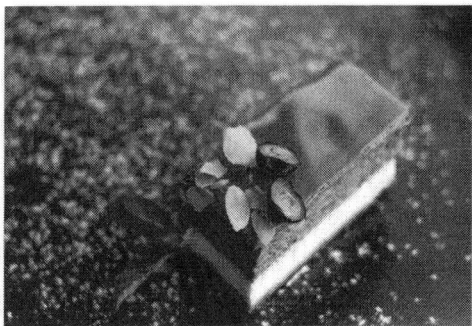

Time: 45 minutes

Serving Size: 16 bars

Ingredients for the crust:

- 1 tsp lemon zest
- 6 tbsp butter (melted)
- ⅓ cup erythritol (granulated)
- 2 cups almond flour (blanched, superfine)

Ingredients for the filling:

- 1 tbsp lemon juice (fresh)
- ½ cup erythritol (granulated)
- 2 cups cream cheese (full-fat)
- 2 big eggs

Ingredients for the swirl:

- 1 tbsp erythritol (granulated)
- ½ cup blueberries (fresh)

Directions:

- Preheat your oven to 350 °F and use parchment paper to line a baking pan.
- In a bowl, combine all of the crust ingredients and mix well.
- Pour the crust batter into the baking pan you have prepared then press it down firmly into the bottom.
- Place the baking pan in the oven and bake the crust for about 8 minutes.
- Take the baking pan out of the oven and allow the crust to cool.
- In a blender, combine all of the filling ingredients and blend until you get a smooth consistency.
- Pour the filling over the cooled crust and use a spatula to spread it evenly.
- In a blender, combine the swirl ingredients and blend until you get a nice consistency.
- Drop spoonfuls of the blueberry mixture into the filling.
- Use a knife to swirl the blueberry mixture into the filling and distribute it.
- Place the baking pan back in the oven and bake the dessert bars for about 25 minutes.
- Take the baking pan out of the oven and allow to cool. Place in the refrigerator to chill for 2 hours before slicing into squares.

Candied Almonds

These crunchy and sweet keto-friendly almonds are so addictive! They're simple to make, and you can make them in batches to enjoy for days to come, even on-the-go!

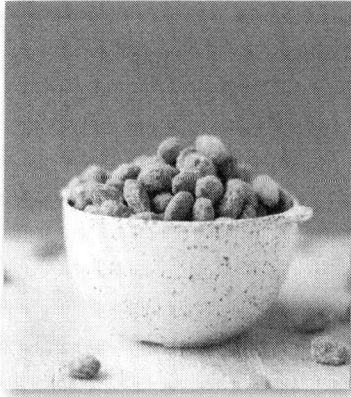

Time: 45 minutes

Serving Size: 12 servings

Ingredients:

- 1 tbsp cinnamon (ground)
- 3 tbsp water
- ¾ keto-friendly sweetener
- 4 cups almonds
- 1 egg (white only)
- salt

Directions:

- Preheat your oven to 250 °F and use parchment paper to line a baking pan.
- In a bowl, combine the cinnamon, sweetener, water, and almonds then mix well.
- In a bowl, combine the egg with a pinch of salt and mix until you get a foamy mixture.
- Add to the nuts and mix well to incorporate.
- Transfer the mixed ingredients to the baking sheet and spread out evenly.
- Place the baking sheet in the oven and bake the nuts for about 35 to 40 minutes. Every 10 minutes or so, open the oven and stir the nuts around.
- Take the baking sheet out of the oven and transfer the nuts to a lined cookie sheet to dry out and cool.
- Once completely cooled, transfer the nuts in an airtight container.

Cheesecake Fat Bombs

These fat bombs are little bites of heaven. Your taste buds will thank you for learning how to make them. And the best part is—these fat bombs don't contain any carbs!

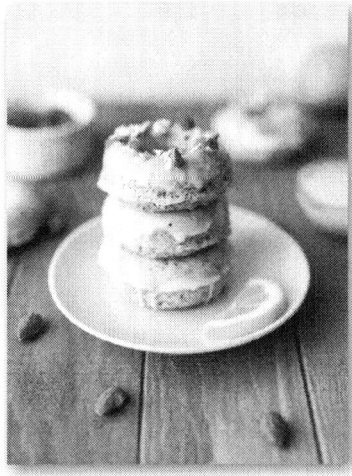

Time: 15 minutes

Serving Size: 24 fat bombs

Ingredients:

- 2 tsp vanilla extract
- 2 tbsp erythritol
- ½ cup butter (melted)
- ½ cup coconut oil
- 1 cup cream cheese
- baking chocolate (grated, for garnish)

Directions:

- In a bowl, combine all of the ingredients and use an electric mixer to beat for about 1 to 2 minutes until you get a creamy mixture.
- Spoon the mixture into a mini cupcake pan.
- Place the mini cupcake pan in the refrigerator for about 2 hours to set.
- Take the mini cupcake pan out of the refrigerator and transfer the fat bombs into an airtight container.

Choco-Hazelnut Tarts

These luscious tarts are perfect for a light and satis-fying snack. It's a high-fat treat with a creamy filling that's out of this world. You can have it for dessert too!

Time: 10 minutes

Serving Size: 8 mini tarts

Ingredients:

- 2 tbsp coconut cream (melted)
- 2 tbsp coconut oil (melted)
- ¼ cup 100% chocolate (sugar-free, melted)
- ¼ cup hazelnut butter
- 8 mini pie crusts (keto-friendly, ready-made)
- erythritol

Directions:

- In a bowl, combine the coconut cream, coconut oil, chocolate, and a pinch of erythritol.

- Spoon hazelnut butter into each of the mini tart crusts.
- Pour the chocolate mixture over the hazelnut butter all the way to the top.
- Place the mini tarts in the refrigerator for about 2 hours to set.

Coconut Blondies

These chewy and moist blondies are tasty and the perfect snack for coconut lovers as they contain coconut in different forms. Learn how to make this recipe now!

Time: 25 minutes

Serving Size: 8 blondies

Ingredients:

- 1 tsp of baking powder
- 2 tsp vanilla extract
- ¼ cup coconut (unsweetened, desiccated)
- ¼ cup coconut cream
- ¼ cup keto-friendly sweetener
- ⅓ cup coconut oil (melted)
- ½ cup coconut flour
- 3 large eggs

Directions:

- Preheat your oven to 350 °F and use parchment paper to line a baking pan.
- In a food processor, combine the vanilla

extract, coconut cream, coconut oil, and eggs then blend until you get a smooth consistency.

- Add the baking powder, coconut, sweetener, and coconut flour then continue blending until you get a smooth batter.
- Pour batter into the baking pan and sprinkle with more shredded coconut.
- Place the baking pan in the oven and bake the blondies for about 20 minutes.
- Take the baking pan out of the oven and allow the blondies to cool down completely before cutting.

Deconstructed Waffle Cone

While ice cream and popsicles are great for dessert, this recipe is an excellent snack that will satisfy your sweet tooth. This is an impressive dish that's simple and satisfying.

Time: 20 minutes

Serving Size: 6 servings

Ingredients for the sauce:

- 1 tsp vanilla extract
- ¼ cup chocolate (unsweetened, finely chopped)
- ⅓ cup keto-friendly sweetener (liquid)
- ¾ cup heavy cream

Ingredients for the waffles:

- ¼ tsp salt (fine)
- ¾ tsp of baking powder
- 2 tsp vanilla extract
- 2 tbsp egg white protein powder
- ¼ cup of cocoa powder (unsweetened)
- ¼ cup of coconut oil

- ¼ cup keto-friendly sweetener (powdered)
- 4 large eggs
- 4 eggs (hard-boiled)
- vanilla bean ice cream (homemade)

Directions:

- Boil water in a pot then bring the heat down to simmer gently.
- In a bowl, combine the chocolate, sweetener, and heavy cream then place on top of the pot with simmering water.
- Stir the ingredients constantly to melt the chocolate and incorporate well.
- Add the vanilla extract, mix well, and place the bowl over warm water to prevent the sauce from cooling down.
- Preheat your waffle iron on high.
- In a blender, combine salt, baking powder, protein powder, cocoa powder, sweetener, raw eggs, and hard-boiled eggs then blend until you get a thick and smooth texture.
- Add the vanilla extract and blend for 30 more seconds.
- Use coconut oil to grease your waffle iron, pour some batter in the middle, and close. Cook batter for about 3 to 4 minutes then transfer to a plate. Repeat until you've finished all of the batter.
- Assemble your deconstructed waffle cone. Start with the waffle, top it off with homemade ice cream (you can use any of the other ice cream flavors you learned how to make too), and drizzle with chocolate sauce.

Fudge Brownie Bites

There's something so comforting and exquisite about biting into a brownie that's warm, soft, and chocolatey. Here's a keto-brownie recipe you can start making right now.

Time: 15 minutes
Serving Size: 6 muffin bites

Ingredients:

- 1 tsp vanilla extract
- ½ cup butter (melted)
- ½ cup erythritol
- ¾ cup almond flour
- ¾ cup cacao powder (unsweetened)
- 2 eggs (whisked)
- salt

Directions:

- Preheat your oven to 350 °F and use parchment paper to line a mini muffin tray.

- In a bowl, combine all of the ingredients and mix well.
- Pour batter into the muffin tray you have prepared.
- Place the muffin tray in the oven and bake for about 13 minutes for a texture that's soft and fudgy. For a cake-like texture, bake for an additional 3 to 5 minutes.
- Take the muffin tray out of the oven and allow the brownie bites to cool down slightly before serving.

Macaroon Fat Bombs

These macaroons are perfect for your keto diet because they're fat bombs too! Snacking on these will add some healthy fats into your daily diet so snack away!

Time: 15 minutes

Serving Size: 10 macaroons

Ingredients:

- 1 tbsp coconut oil
- 1 tbsp vanilla extract
- 2 tbsp keto-friendly sweetener
- ½ cup coconut (shredded)
- ¼ almond flour (organic)
- 3 eggs (whites only)

Directions:

- Preheat your oven to 350 °F and use parchment paper to line a muffin tray.
- Place a bowl in the freezer to chill.

- In a separate bowl, combine the sweetener, coconut, and almond flour then mix well.
- In a saucepan, combine coconut oil and vanilla extract then heat until melted and blended.
- Take the saucepan off the heat and pour the mixture into the bowl with dry ingredients and blend until well incorporated.
- Take the chilled bowl out of the freezer, add the eggs, and whisk until you form very stiff peaks.
- Gently add the egg whites into the batter being careful not to overmix.
- Spoon the batter into the muffin tray, place it in the oven and bake the macaroons for about 8 minutes.
- Take the muffin tray out of the oven and allow the macaroons to cool down.

Mini Lemon and Blackberry Tarts

As soon as berry season comes along, you can make these scrumptious tarts. These mini tarts are simple, healthy, and serve as a filling and satisfying snack for all occasions.

Time: 2 hours

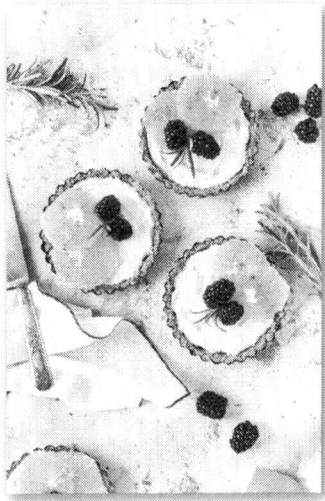

Serving Size: 10 mini tarts

Ingredients for the crust:

- ¾ cup coconut (shredded)
- 1 cup macadamia nuts
- 1 big egg

Ingredients for the filling:

- ⅕ tsp keto-friendly sweetener (liquid)
- 1 tbsp gelatin powder

- 2 tbsp water
- ¼ cup erythritol (powdered)
- 1 cup of coconut milk
- ½ lemon (juiced)
- ½ lemon (zest)

Ingredients for the topping:

- 1 cup blackberries (fresh)

Directions:

- In a saucepan, add the coconut milk and heat on low heat.
- Add the lemon juice, lemon zest, erythritol, and sweetener. Mix together well and bring the mixture to a boil. Once it boils, take the saucepan off the heat.
- Combine the water and gelatin, mix well, and add to the heated mixture. Continue mixing until dissolved then set aside to thicken while cooling down.
- Preheat your oven to 350 °F and grease a mini muffin tray.
- In a blender, add the macadamia nuts and pulse until you get the consistency you desire. Transfer the nuts into a bowl.
- In the same blender, add the coconut and pulse again until you get the consistency you desire. Add to the bowl along with the egg and mix together until well combined.
- Pour batter into a muffin tray you have prepared, just enough to serve as the crust for

your tarts. Also, make sure to spread the batter evenly.

- Place the muffin tray in the oven and bake the crust for about 7 to 10 minutes.
- Take the muffin tray out of the oven and allow the crusts to cool down.
- Spoon filling into the mini tarts, add a few blueberries and place them in the refrigerator for about 30 to 60 minutes to set.

Peanut Butter and Chocolate Bark with Pecans

This carb-free peanut butter and chocolate treat is perfect for late-night snacking. It's dairy-free, gluten-free, and you can omit the nuts easily if you have a nut allergy.

Time: 1 hour

Serving Size: 1 batch

Ingredients:

- ¼ tsp sea salt
- 1 tsp almond extract
- 1 tsp vanilla extract
- ¼ cup cacao powder (unsweetened)
- ½ cup coconut (unsweetened, shredded)
- ½ cup keto-friendly sweetener
- ½ cup peanut butter (creamy)
- 1 cup of coconut oil
- nuts of your choice (optional)

Directions:

- In a saucepan, combine the peanut butter and coconut oil, heat, and stir gently until completely melted and you get a creamy consistency.
- Take the saucepan off the heat and transfer the mixture to a bowl.
- Add the sea salt, vanilla extract, almond extract, cacao powder, coconut, sweetener, and nuts if desired then mix well.
- Use a sheet of parchment paper to line a baking sheet then pour the mixture into it.
- Place the baking sheet in the oven and freeze the chocolate for about 1 hour.
- Once solid, break the chocolate bark into pieces and store in an airtight container.

Peppermint Patties

These easy peppermint patties are so simple, but they will make your taste buds dance and your heart sing. They're sugar and dairy-free making them a healthy snack.

Time: 25 minutes
Serving Size: 12 peppermint patties

Ingredients:

- 1 ½ tsp peppermint extract
- 1 tbsp cocoa butter
- 2 tbsp coconut cream
- ¼ cup dark chocolate (sugar-free, chopped)
- ½ cup coconut oil (softened slightly)
- ½ cup keto-friendly sweetener (powdered)

Directions:

- In a bowl, combine the coconut cream and coconut oil then beat until you get a smooth consistency.
- Add the peppermint extract and sweetener then continue mixing.
- Use a sheet of parchment paper to line a baking sheet. Spoon a heaping teaspoon of the mixture onto the baking sheet and spread gently to

form a circle. Repeat until you've used up the whole mixture.

- Place the baking sheet in the refrigerator for about 2 hours until firm.
- In a pot, bring water to a boil. Then turn the heat down low, allowing the water to simmer gently.
- In a bowl, combine the cacao butter and chocolate. Place the bowl on top of the pot and stir the mixture until the chocolate melts. Take the bowl off the heat.
- Take the baking sheet out of the oven and dip the patties into the chocolate mixture one at a time until they are all fully coated.
- Return to the baking sheet and allow to set before serving.

Piña Colada Fat Bombs

These low-carb fat bombs will bring back memories of lovely summer flavors. Unlike the cocktail, this recipe doesn't contain alcohol or sugar—but they're really tasty!

Time: 1 hour and 10 minutes

Serving Size: 16 fat bombs

Ingredients:

- 1 tsp rum extract
- 2 tsp pineapple essence
- 3 tsp erythritol
- 2 tbsp gelatin
- ½ cup coconut cream
- ½ cup water (boiling)
- 2 scoops MCT (powdered, optional)

Directions:

- In a heatproof jug, add the boiling water then dissolve the erythritol and gelatin. Add pineapple essence and mix well.

- Set aside to cool for about 5 minutes.
- Add the rum extract and coconut cream then continue stirring for another 2 minutes. Mix in the MCT powder if desired.
- Pour mixture into silicone molds and allow to set for 1 hour or until firm.

Zabaglione With Meringues

This sweet snack might seem indecently sweet and indulgent—but as with the other recipes in this book, it fits right into your keto diet. It's just designed to taste amazing!

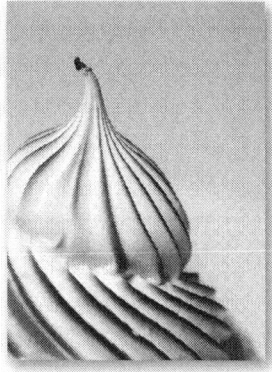

Time: 3 hours

Serving Size: 6 servings

Ingredients:

- ⅕ tsp keto-friendly sweetener (powdered)
- 2 tsp vanilla extract (divided)
- 4 tbsp coconut oil
- 1 cup heavy whipping cream
- 1 lemon (zest only)
- 1 stick of butter (organic)
- 3 medium-sized strawberries (organic)
- 6 medium-sized eggs (organic, separated)

Directions:

- Place a bowl in the freezer to chill.
- Preheat your oven to 200 °F and use parchment paper to line a cookie sheet.
- In a bowl, combine the vanilla extract, half of the sweetener, and the egg whites. Use a hand mixer on low to whip everything together for 30 seconds. Then turn up the speed on high until mixture forms stiff peaks.
- Separate ⅓ of the egg white mixture and set aside.
- For the rest of the egg white mixture, spoon it into a pastry bag with a big nozzle.
- Squeeze out mounds of egg white mixture onto the cookie sheet you have prepared.
- Place the cookie sheet in the oven and bake the meringue for about 3 hours with the oven's door slightly ajar.
- In a pot, bring water to a boil. Then turn the heat down low allowing the water to simmer gently.
- In a bowl, combine the butter and coconut oil. Place the bowl on top of the pot and stir the mixture until the ingredients melt and are well incorporated.
- In a blender, combine the vanilla extract, strawberries, lemon zest, and the rest of the stevia blend to incorporate.
- In the bowl with the butter and coconut oil, add the egg yolks and mix well until you get a foamy and smooth consistency.
- Add the strawberry mixture as you continue

mixing gently. Then add the egg white mixture and continue mixing until well incorporated.

- Cook all of the ingredients for about 5 minutes as you stir constantly to ensure that it doesn't stick to the sides or bottom of the bowl.
- When you have a frothy and light consistency, take the bowl off the heat and set aside.
- Take the bowl you have chilled out of the freezer and add the heavy cream.
- Use a hand mixer set on high and whip until you form stiff peaks.
- Assemble your zabaglione. Start by spooning the zabaglione mixture into glasses, top with whipped cream, and meringue.

CONCLUSION:
Enjoying Desserts on the Keto Diet

THE KETOGENIC DIET is a low-carb, high-fat diet that allows you to enjoy a wide variety of foods while eliminating others from your diet. When you go keto, you have to reduce your carb and sugar intake drastically—but this doesn't mean you have to say goodbye to desserts forever. As you have learned all throughout this book, it's all about learning how to choose keto-friendly ingredients.

In this book, you have learned a lot of dessert recipes that are easy, healthy, and oh-so-delicious. We've gone through recipes for cookies, cakes, cupcakes, muffins, ice cream, popsicles, pudding, mousse, sweet bread, sweet loaf, pizzas, bars, crepes, and even a couple of sweet snack suggestions. All of these recipes contain keto-friendly ingredients making it simpler for you to follow them. Actually, these recipes are similar to traditional recipes—the only difference is that we have already replaced the non-keto ingredients with keto-friendly ones.

After some practice, you will be able to perform the substitutions and adjustments yourself. You can apply this same method with other recipes too, not just desserts. Cooking is a fun, pleasurable, and satisfying activity which is why you should make it a part of your life, especially as a keto dieter. When you make your own desserts (and meals), you know exactly what goes into them. You can enjoy them guilt-free without wondering if what you're eating is truly keto-friendly or not.

With that being said... what are you waiting for! It's time to start creating your own homemade desserts to enjoy after your meals or any time you're craving for something sweet and keto-friendly. Have fun!